You W<u> </u>be Left Behind!

Essays on the Bible and 'End Times' Teachings

JM Smith

"Dojo Discussions" Series

http://jmsmith.org

2

Contents

-Introduction-

My first exposure to the topic of the "End Times" came when I was in the 8ᵗʰ grade. My Dad—I'm a preacher's kid—taught a study of the book of Revelation to our middle school Sunday School class. He used the video series "Breaking the Code" by Bruce Metzger and I'm probably the only one in that class who even remembers anything about it. Esteemed New Testament manuscript experts with silver hair and a somewhat sedated speaking style don't really capture the imaginations of most 8ᵗʰ graders.

I was the exception, I guess.

I loved how Metzger pulled back the veil on what was, until then in my mind, an incomprehensible book tucked away at the end of the Bible. In the 20+ years since that class, Revelation has not only become my favorite New Testament book to teach on, but I've also maintained a large amount of respect for Metzger's contributions to my study and growth, despite no longer agreeing with everything he taught in that study.

My next exposure to eschatology (a fancy seminary word that just means "study of things related to the end") came later that same year at a lock-in. To this day, I cannot

6

figure out why we loved lock-ins so much as kids—the thought of having to stay up all night as an adult is now torturous! But as a middle schooler, lock-ins were the greatest things ever! This one was the first we had under a new Youth Director who the church had just hired and, as usually happens at lock-ins, around 3am it was time for a movie.

The movie that our new leader chose was the classic masterpiece "A Thief in the Night" ...seriously. That's what we watched.

Now I'm sure a number of you have seen this cinematic gem...but for those who haven't, it's part of a genre of poorly-made Christian films (I know, I know, that's somewhat redundant) made during the "Rapture craze" in the 1970s that were fueled in large part by Hal Lindsay's best-selling "The Late Great Planet Earth" and meant to scare viewers by showing them the horrors of life on earth if they miss the Rapture—when Jesus returns invisibly and takes all true believers out of the world before the Great Tribulation of God's judgment which will last for seven years. After that, Jesus will return (visibly this time) and inaugurate His worldwide utopian kingdom from a throne in Jerusalem that lasts for a thousand years.

The movie was so bad that I couldn't take it seriously (this was the early 90s, when movies like Terminator 2 and Jurassic Park were setting the bar for Hollywood special effects after all!). But despite having heard about it from various youth speakers and Baptist friends, it just seemed so at odds with everything else I knew about the Bible.

Looking back, I can see that this is because...well...it was.

But it would be nearly 10 years before I'd give it any serious thought. In the meantime, I just chalked it up to being one of the many things we'll never understand fully and went on about my business.

But in college, as I began studying Scripture more seriously, the whole "Left Behind" approach continued to seem more and more out of line with what I was reading in the Bible. The TV preachers and "prophecy experts" with their insanely-detailed full-color charts and their newspaper headline clippings sounded confident...but also very wrong to me.

When I got to seminary at Gordon-Conwell in the Fall of 2001, I had a fairly good grasp of basic theological traditions and a solid understanding of apologetics—I had been forced to hone my apologetic knowledge during the year of open-air preaching on campus I did when I worked for the Wesley Foundation (a whole other story for another time, perhaps!). But where I was totally lacking was in the area of eschatology. I knew there were a number of different positions Christians held; but I didn't know much about them other than the very basics of each view (Premillennial, Amillennial, Postmillennial, etc.). I began studying Greek and New Testament interpretation, as well as Systematic Theology. After that, came Summer Hebrew. Then, during my second year I took "Exegesis of Revelation" with Sean McDonough.

That was the best New Testament class I ever took.

Dr. McDonough walked us through not only the book of Revelation, but also the various ways it had been studied and interpreted over the centuries. By that time, I had read enough theology and Biblical studies to realize that the system of eschatology upon which things like "The Late Great Planet Earth", "A Thief in the Night", and the "Left Behind" franchise were based was a mid-19th century invention that no Christian had ever taught before then. Despite the grassroots popularity of this approach—fueled by early 20th century

"Prophecy Conferences", the Scofield Study Bible, correspondence courses from Bible colleges, winsome evangelists with scary full-color charts, two World Wars, and the rise of Christian satellite TV—the idea of "the rapture" and its accompanying theological framework of interpreting bits of Scripture together in a "literal" and "scientific" manner was one that the larger worldwide historic Christian Church had never embraced.

Dr. McDonough had us translate the entire book from the Greek text and then choose a particular passage to thoroughly exegete (both my translation and my exegesis of my chosen passage are included in the appendices at the end of this book). This enabled me to see what Revelation in particular, and eschatology as a whole, were really all about. It helped me to see the different ways people have approached this enigmatic book throughout history (or, in the case of Calvin and Wesley, intentionally refused to write much about it due to their admitted incomprehension!) and to better identify the various strengths and weaknesses of all the different views surrounding the subject.

It also drilled into my spirit the MASSIVE NEED for the Church worldwide to recover the message of Revelation and the overall big picture of the Bible's teaching about things related to the "End Times." There is SO MUCH floating around out there that is at best misguided and at worst dangerously deceptive when it comes to eschatology...particularly when eschatological views come up against modern geopolitical realities that affect real people on the ground. Nowhere is this more graphically illustrated than within the ongoing Israeli-Palestinian conflict and the division within the Church worldwide over the details surrounding it (which will be discussed in more detail below).

Then, few years ago I started Disciple Dojo for the purpose of teaching and equipping Christians in their understanding of Scripture and how one's theological outlook intersects with the world around them. I knew that one of the main areas of study I wanted to help the Church worldwide in was eschatology. To that end, I produced a DVD curriculum which walks readers through the book of Revelation chapter by chapter entitled "Revelation: A Guided Tour of the Apocalypse".

But I knew that eschatology was much broader than the pages of that final book of the Bible...it started all the way back in Genesis and runs like a thread through every page of Scripture.

Something more was needed.

I had also been getting a lot of questions about things related to End Times, the Rapture, modern day Israel, the antichrist, and all the other questions that capture the popular imagination (both within and outside of the church's walls!). So when my friend and Discipleship Director, Chris Thayer, asked me if I'd teach a class at Good Shepherd, I thought this would be the perfect opportunity to put together a comprehensive study of all things related to the Bible and the "End Times." The result was "Apocalypse Now?? What the Bible Teaches About the End Times", a 10-week series of audio lectures on CD. I also decided that I would give it away for free in MP3 format so that as many people as possible could have access to something other than the typical pop-theology which dominates North American evangelical culture (click on the Podcast link at the top of http://jmsmith.org to listen and/or download the entire series for free and be sure to share it with others all over the world!).

This book is intended to be a supplement to that series of lectures. Though you can read this as a stand-alone book of essays and discussions, and hopefully learn a good deal from it, for fuller discussion of many terms used throughout it and a deeper look at various sections of Scripture we will be discussing, the interested reader is STRONGLY encouraged to either download or buy the "Apocalypse Now??" lectures.

Lastly, I want to thank some of the people who have shaped my understanding and sharpened my thinking in this area:

My Dad, Rev. Jim Smith – For instilling a hunger to study and proclaim the meaning found in Scripture even when it's not popular and for raising me to be one who always questions what I think I already know by listening to multiple voices from various traditions and viewpoints. I also want to thank my wonderful Mom, Diane Smith, who has not only been a lifelong encourager and amazing Mother to me and my Sister, but who also was kind enough to edit this book and catch most of my typos!

My Biblical Studies professors at Gordon-Conwell (both in South Hamilton and Charlotte) particularly Sean McDonough (his passion when teaching Revelation was a thing of beauty), Walt Kaiser, Jeff Niehaus, Doug Stuart, Tim Laniak, Gary Pratico and Gordon Hugenberger – For setting the bar high and demonstrating a gracious ecumenical approach without requiring uniformity of thought.

The scholars whose work I have benefited so much from over the years through their commentaries, articles and monographs. In particular (and in no particular order): Ben Witherington, N.T. Wright, Christopher Wright, Craig Koester, Greg Beale, Richard Bauckham, Kim Riddlebarger, G.B. Caird, Ian Boxall, Tremper Longman, Robert Lowry, Paul Spilsbury and Craig Keener.

And lastly, to the followers of Jesus in *both* Israel and Palestine who are often caught in the middle of decades of hatred, fear, ethnic/religious tribalism and oppression in their own land by the extremists who thrive on such things. You are not overlooked by the eyes of the One Seated on the Throne...in fact, I believe you together (Jew and Arab!) are the primary means by which His Kingdom will overcome and put all things right when all's said and done. May you persevere in following the Slaughtered Lamb, no matter what you face in response.

Blessings from the Dojo,

JM Smith
November, 2012

-One-
Are Things Just Getting Worse and Worse?

"Our culture is so depraved!"

"We've turned away from God!"

"We're rushing toward total moral decay at an unprecedented rate!"

"Weren't we better off in the days when we were a God-fearing society??"

Whenever I encounter these or similar sentiments by well-meaning Christians, my answer is usually unexpected:

> "Actually, no, I don't believe things are not really getting worse. This world is no more fallen now than it's ever been in the past."

Usually the "our-culture-is-heading-headlong-into-hell-in-a-hand-basket" (alliteration is fun!) line of argument is made by those who long for "the good ol' days"...

You know, usually sometime around the 1930s-1950s...

When there was also:

- a Great Depression
- Multiple World Wars
- Massive genocide throughout Europe (and elsewhere)
- Global unchecked nuclear proliferation
- and let's not forget about good ol' Jim Crowe segregation laws!

No, today's culture is not any worse now that it's ever been. At least, I'm not convinced that it is.

In fact, when I read through the pages of the Hebrew Bible (or as Christians call it, the Old Testament), I see such things as government-mandated fertility goddess orgies and child sacrifice (e.g. Canaan)!

And in the New Testament, I see state-sponsored-mandatory-polytheism (e.g. Pergamum) and Imperial slavery (e.g. Rome)!

And that's just scratching the surface! To get a fuller picture, read the Hebrew Prophets, Paul's letters to the Corinthian Christians, and Jesus' Revelation to His Church (aka. the last book in the Bible)...you'll see evils on a scale we can hardly imagine—both outside of AND within the community of God's People!

We Christians in the US, particularly here in the Bible belt, who feel that we're so much worse off now than in the past need to ask ourselves two questions:

> 1. How many more believers are there in the world today than there ever have been who are advancing the Kingdom of God?

> 2. When's the last time you were required by the local government to take part in a pagan feast and/or ritual sex in honor of the local gods and goddesses?

It seems to me that good and evil, sin and righteousness, justice and oppression have ALWAYS been part of this fallen world and have been equally prevalent in every age. It also seems that in every age, there are those who long for "the good ol' days."

Need proof?

Listen to this critique of current youth culture:

> "*I see no hope for the future of our people if they depend on the frivolous youth of today, for certainly all youth are reckless beyond words. When I was a boy we were taught to be discreet and respectful of elders, but the present youth are exceedingly wild and impatient of restraint!*"

18

Sounds pretty familiar, huh?

Did it come from a Conservative news pundit, Televangelist, or Sunday School teacher here in 21st century America?

Nope.

The person who is reported to have uttered that quote was actually the Greek poet Hesiod...who lived about 700 years before Jesus' birth![1]

I suspect though, that people will always feel this way...

...culture is spiraling out of control.

...things are worse now than ever before.

... young people are growing up in a moral abyss.

Such sentiments will be held by many Christians until Jesus returns and "puts the

---

[1] Admittedly, there is some dispute as to whether or not Hesiod actually said this. However, it certainly reflects similar views of "youth culture" held by many of the ancients, so it serves as helpful illustration of the main point—the "good ol' days" belong to a non-existent past that everyone seems to long for, but no one seems to have experienced! For more on the quote source, see: http://www.englishforums.com/English/HelpSourceQuotation/wjnqm/post.htm

world to rights once and for all" (as N.T. Wright puts it[2]).

So what do we do in the meantime??

I believe we must continue to live somewhere between the Religious Fundamentalists' gloom-and-doom outlook and the Religious Liberals' naive optimism regarding the ability of the noble human spirit. God's truth is almost always somewhere in the middle of extremes.

Lord, help us stay balanced in this life you've called us to.

---

[2] See the article by Wright at :
http://www.spu.edu/depts/uc/response/summer2k5/features/evil.asp

-Two-
Why According to Jesus...
You WANT to Be 'Left Behind'!

"When Jesus comes back, you don't want to be left behind, do you??"

This question has been asked countless times by countless sincere Christians to those with whom they are sharing the Gospel. The implied answer is, "Of course not! You want to be taken up in the Rapture and avoid the horrors of the Great Tribulation!"

However, what many of my evangelical brothers and sisters are often unaware of is that the answer to this question should be *the exact opposite* of the one they are hoping to hear!

Wait...what??

Let's look at Jesus' actual words from the passage that is the sole source for the famous notion of being "left behind":

> *"No one knows about that day or hour, not even the angels in heaven, nor the Son, but only the Father. As it was in the days of Noah, so it will be at the coming of the Son of Man. For in the days before*

> *the flood, people were eating and drinking, marrying and giving in marriage, up to the day Noah entered the ark; and they knew nothing about what would happen until the flood came and took them all away. That is how it will be at the coming of the Son of Man. Two men will be in the field; one will be taken and the other left. Two women will be grinding with a hand mill; one will be taken and the other left. Therefore keep watch, because you do not know on what day your Lord will come."* (Matthew 24:36-42)

This passage and its parallels are part of the "Olivet Discourse"—the speech Jesus gave to His disciples on the Mount of Olives across from and overlooking Jerusalem during the days just before His crucifixion. And there are a number of factors which determine how Christians will interpret this famous discourse...such as to what exactly the "coming" of the Son of Man is actually referring. (See the chapter below on Jesus' prediction of the Temple's destruction for more on this!)

But for argument's sake, let's assume that Jesus is referring to His return at the end of this age in the Olivet Discourse, and in this passage in Matthew 24, in particular.

Is He saying that He's coming to snatch believers away suddenly and invisibly via "the rapture"?

Will those who are "left" endure the horrible Tribulation and schemes of the (usually European Catholic) Antichrist, such as Tim LaHaye, Hal Lindsay, Jack Van Impe, David Jeremiah, John Hagee, and other "Prophecy Experts" have been warning us about for decades?

The answer to both of these, according to Jesus' very own words, is an emphatic "no."

In fact, I believe that this is easily the most famous (and best-selling!) instance of Biblical *mis*interpretation of all time.

In fact, it is 100% wrong.

Now that's a VERY strong claim, so I'd better be able to back it up! I believe I can. And all that's needed is to look at Jesus' *own words in context*.

Read the passage again. Go ahead. I'll be right here when you get back.

...

Did you catch the comparison Jesus was making?

> *"As it was in the days of Noah...*
> *so it will be at the coming of the Son of*
> *Man..."*

Let's ask just a few simple questions based on this passage:

1. In Noah's day, what did the 'taking'?

According to Jesus, it was the flood.

2. After the flood 'took' everyone who was eating and drinking, marrying and being given in marriage, and didn't know it was coming anyway...who were the ones that were 'left'?

Noah and his family.

3. In Noah's day, would you have wanted to be 'taken' by the flood or 'left'?

You definitely wouldn't want to be taken in God's judgment of the world through the flood!

4. So in this analogy Jesus is using, if this is how it will be when He returns should His followers want to be "taken" or "left"???

> Left...just like Noah and his family!

Notice that we didn't appeal to any Greek grammatical terms or hidden background information. We didn't appeal to any nuanced meanings of obscure terms. We simply read the passage with Jesus' own words in their own context and drew the absolute clearest meaning possible from them, based on the analogy to which He, Himself was appealing (Go back and reread the passage a few times in your own Bible to make sure if you're still not convinced!).

And the result is *the exact opposite* of what most people assume this famous 'left behind' passage actually says.

The fact is Jesus ALWAYS taught that when He returned, He would return in judgment which would consist of evildoers being removed to a place of punishment and everlasting destruction, and the righteous being raised to new, incorruptible, eternal life with Him in the New Heavens and New Earth:

"Again, the kingdom of heaven is like a net that was thrown into the sea and gathered fish of every kind. When it was full, men drew it ashore and sat down and sorted the good into containers but threw away the bad. So it will be at the close of the age. The angels will come out and separate the evil from the righteous and throw them into the fiery furnace. In that place there will be weeping and gnashing of teeth." (Mat 13:47-50 ESV)

Other examples of this same teaching can be seen in the following parables of Jesus:

- The Wheat and the Weeds (Matt. 13:24-30)
- The Sheep and the Goats (Matt. 25:31-46).

The pattern is the same in all of them—when it comes to God's final judgment, being 'taken', 'removed', 'cast out' or 'thrown away' are different ways of referring to the same thing...and it's NEVER a good thing!

So, regardless of what you may hear on TV or an End-Times thriller starring Kirk Cameron, Gary Bussey, or (I kid you not) Nicholas Cage, remember the basic message of Jesus on the subject.

According to *Jesus Himself*, YOU WANT TO BE LEFT BEHIND.

The alternative is God's Judgment of the wicked...something I hope no one reading this will ever experience.

-Three-
Why *The Rapture* is What REALLY Should Be 'Left Behind'!

The doctrine of The Rapture is one that even most non-Christians are familiar with--thanks in part to bumper stickers, t-shirts, and the pop-Christian-culture success of books like Hal Lindsay's "*The Late Great Planet Earth*" and the multimillion dollar "*Left Behind*" franchise by Tim LaHaye and Jerry Jenkins.

Given all of the above, it's not surprising that most people--Christian and non-Christian alike--believe that the Bible clearly and unambiguously teaches that at some point in the future Jesus will make a partial return to earth to snatch believers away in a massive, invisible, worldwide disappearance, leaving behind empty cars, cribs, planes and "In-case-of-rapture-this-shirt-will-be-unmanned" t-shirts! There was even a company started by non-Christians with which those waiting to be raptured could register in order to have someone take care of their pets once they themselves have been whisked away. I'm not making this up. If you don't believe me check out http://eternal-earthbound-pets.com !

But it may come as a surprise to many readers to find out that Bible does not, in fact, teach anything of the sort!

Having just looked at the only passage in Scripture where the famous "Left Behind" concept comes from, and seeing that Jesus was actually saying the EXACT OPPOSITE of what most people assume, let's now look at the most popular passage in Scripture that people who advocate belief in the rapture rely upon. It comes from the letter Paul wrote to the Christians in Thessalonica:

> Brothers, we do not want you to be ignorant about those who fall asleep, or to grieve like the rest of men, who have no hope. We believe that Jesus died and rose again and so we believe that God will bring with Jesus those who havefallen asleep in him.

> According to the Lord's own word, we tell you that we who are still alive, who are left till the coming of the Lord, will certainly not precede those who have fallen asleep. For the Lord himself will come down from heaven, with a loud command, with the voice of the archangel and with the trumpet call of God, and the dead in Christ will rise first.

After that, we who are still alive and are left will be caught up together with them in the clouds to meet the Lord in the air. And so we will be with the Lord forever. Therefore encourage each other with these words. (1Thessalonians 4:13-18)

This passage is, in fact, where the term "rapture" comes from.

The word translated "*caught up*" in Greek is "*harpazo*". When the New Testament was translated into Latin, the word "*rapiemur*", which means "*to be snatched up*" was used to render it.

It is from this verb that we get the English term "rapture".

But does this being "*caught up*" really refer to Christians being whisked away into the clouds in a massive disappearance act, leaving behind a confused world that will then go through 7 years of horrible tribulation until a final Antichrist figure emerges (from somewhere in Europe, according to most versions of Rapture theology!) and attempts to destroy the city of Jerusalem in a massive Chinese/Russian/Iraqi/Iranian invasion--only to be stopped by Jesus' visible return to reign on earth for 1000 years from a throne in

Jerusalem?? (Whew! That's a lot to recount in a single paragraph!)

In short...it does not.

And what most people also don't realize is that historically speaking, Christians have never believed this to be to what this passage is referring!

Only in the 1850s did this view begin to emerge. It later became entrenched within American Fundamentalism and Evangelicalism via the Scofield Reference Bible study notes as well as the teaching of institutions such as Moody Bible College and Dallas Theological Seminary.[3]

[*For more on the historical development of this view of the End Times, be sure to check out* the series of lectures from Disciple Dojo's audio course entitled "Apocalypse Now??" available for online in both streaming and download format at http://sermon.net/jmsmith or on CDs at http://jmsmith.org/store/apocalypse]

But the historical Christian Church worldwide has not believed that Paul is referring to any future mass disappearance of Christians from all over the globe.

---

[3] See Robert Lowry's summary at: http://rlowery.com/2009/03/02/a-century-of-damage/

Rather, he is talking about the final return of Jesus as conquering King and Judge of the Living and Dead. And he is doing so using the unmistakable vocabulary of Roman Imperial rhetoric, which his Thessalonian readers would've immediately recognized. New Testament scholar Ben Witherington elaborates (I'm quoting at length so readers can follow Witherington's full train of thought):

> [W]hat sort of return is Paul envisioning here? Can it be a secret or invisible return? Do we have some sort of theology of a pre-tribulation rapture here with Jesus not actually coming to earth? The details of the text as well as the use of the language of the royal visit to a city surely rule out such a view....V. 16 also makes as clear as one could want that we are dealing with a public event, one announced not only by a loud command, as on a battlefield, and the voice of the archangel, but also by the trumpet call of God, though these may be three ways of referring to the same sound. The images are martial, as if Jesus were summoning his army.

> The meeting place is said to take place in the clouds or in the air, not in heaven. Paul considers the dead in Christ to be

persons who can be "awakened" or "addressed." He is probably drawing on the *yom Yahweh* ["Day of the LORD"] traditions, which referred to a trumpet blast announcing the event (cf. Isa. 27:13; Joel 2:1; Zech. 9:14; 1 Cor. 15:52). But it was also the case that a royal visit to a city would be announced by a herald (see Ps. 24:7–10) and might well also be announced by a trumpet blast meant to alert those in the city that the king was coming.

This imagery is pursued further in v. 17 with the use of the term *apantesin* ["to meet"]. For example, Cicero says of Julius Caesar's victory tour through Italy in 49 b.c.: "*Just imagine what a meeting/royal welcome (apantesis) he is receiving from the towns, what honors are paid to him*" (Ad. Atticus 8.16.2). **This word refers, then, to the actions of the greeting committee as it goes forth from the city to escort the royal person or dignitary into the city for his official visit.** "These analogies (especially in association with the term *parousia* ["presence/arrival"]) suggest the possibility that the Lord is pictured here as escorted the remainder of the journey to earth by his people—both those newly raised from the dead and those remaining alive.

[Church Father John] Chrysostom picked up these nuances quite clearly:

> *"For when a king drives into a city, those who are honorable go out to meet him; but the condemned await the judge within. And upon the coming of an affectionate father, his children indeed, and those who are worthy to be his children, are taken out in a chariot, that they may see him and kiss him; but the housekeepers who have offended him remain within.* (Homily 8 on 1 Thessalonians)"

Paul's Thessalonian audience may have missed some of the allusions to the Old Testament, but they would not have missed the language used here about a royal visit, indeed an imperial visit. They would remember the visit of Pompey and later Octavian and others in the days when Thessalonike could even be talked about by Pompey as the capital in exile.[4]

---

[4] Witherington, Ben. *1 and 2 Thessalonians : A Socio-Rhetorical Commentary* (Eerdmans, Grand Rapids, 2006).

36

Witherington is not alone in seeing this entire passage as Paul speaking, not of a "rapture", but of a the final return of Jesus, and His followers meeting him (both those who are alive, as well as those who have died and are resurrected) upon His arrival, and welcoming Him as one would welcome a triumphant ruler returning from victorious battle to sit upon his rightful throne. Scholars from many denominations and theological traditions recognize that what is going on in 1Thessalonians 4 is nothing resembling current pop-theology:

> "The picture is that of a group of citizens going out from a city to meet a visiting dignitary and accompany him back. This implies that the Lord returns with his people to the earth. (They certainly do not stay permanently on the clouds playing harps!) This language was probably never intended to be understood absolutely literally; it is describing things that go beyond words. The important thing is that believers, whether the dead or the living, are from then with the Lord for ever."[5]

[5] Carson, D.A. ed. *New Bible Commentary : 21st Century Edition* (Inter-Varsity Press, Downers Grove 1994)

"In describing the second coming of Jesus, Paul uses another cluster of images borrowed from the triumph of the divine warrior. The trumpet call (1 Cor 15:52; 1 Thess 4:16), for example, is reminiscent of the call to battle, just as the picture of the faithful meeting the Lord in the air (1 Thess 4:17) is drawn from the practice of coming out of the city to welcome a returning warrior who has been successful in battle. The use of this cluster of images communicates that Jesus is God's agent of salvation but also defines salvation, in part, as the defeat of Satan (and all that would oppose God's purpose) in cosmic warfare. The book of Revelation, of course, continues the theme of divine warfare in relation to Jesus' return."[6]

"When all the dead in Christ are raised, then the trumpet shall sound, as the signal for them all to flock together to the throne of Christ. It was by the sound of the trumpet that the solemn assemblies, under the law, were convoked; and to such convocations there appears to be here an allusion. When the dead in Christ are raised, their vile bodies being made like unto his

---

[6] Ryken, Leland ed. *The Dictionary of Biblical Imagery* (InterVarsity Press, Downers Grove 1998), 769.

glorious body, then, those who are alive shall be changed, and made immortal. These shall be caught up together with them to meet the Lord in the air. 8. We may suppose that the judgment will now be set, and the books opened, and the dead judged out of the things written in those books. The eternal states of quick and dead being thus determined, then all who shall be found to have made a covenant with him by sacrifice, and to have washed their robes, and made them white in the blood of the Lamb, shall be taken to his eternal glory, and be for ever with the Lord. What an inexpressibly terrific glory will then be exhibited!"[7]

The late British Pastor and Theologian, John R.W. Stott--who is widely considered an "Elder Statesman of Evangelicalism"--sums up the message of this passage beautifully:

"Thus the coming of Jesus, Paul seems to be hinting by the mere adoption of this word, will be a revelation of God and a personal, powerful visitation by Jesus, the King. It can hardly be fortuitous that he is writing this to the Thessalonians

---

[7] Clarke, Adam. *Clarke's Commentary: First Thessalonians* (electronic ed.;, Logos Library System, Ages Software, 1999)

among whom, at least according to his critics, he had defied Claudius Caesar's decrees by announcing 'that there is another king, one called Jesus'.?

The Christian hope, however, is more than the expectation that the King is coming; it is also the belief that when he comes, the Christian dead will come with him and the Christian living will join them. For it is the separation which death causes (or seems to cause) which is so painful, both separation from Christ, since the dead have died before he comes, and separation from those who survive them, since they have gone ahead and left the living behind. It is these two bitter separations which the apostle solemnly assures his readers are neither real nor permanent.   For the dead will come with Jesus, and the living will   not   precede   them.[8]

So, given the fact that neither Jesus nor Paul ever taught that Christians would be "raptured" out of the world before the final return of Christ, and given that the key proof-texts for such a view teach nothing of the sort,

---

[8] Stott, John R.W. *The Message of Thessalonians: The Gospel & the End of Time* (Inter-Varsity Press, Leicester, England, 1994), 97.

perhaps it's time that pop-theologies of an invisible rapture of Christians to Heaven so that the world can perish, are what actually get 'left behind.'

-Four-
Are Recent Natural Disasters
Signs of Jesus' Return?

Whenever a major disaster occurs, one of the first things many Christians do is attempt to correlate it to the end times and the return of Jesus. This is especially true when the event in question is an earthquake (such as the major one that led to the tsunami in Southeast Asia).

Often the passage cited as proof of correlation is the Olivet Discourse spoken by Jesus (as we saw in an earlier chapter, it's called the Olivet Discourse because He spoke it while standing on the Mount of Olives overlooking Jerusalem in the final days of His earthly life).

A form of the discourse appears in all three synoptic Gospels (Matthew 24, Mark 13 and Luke 21) and the key verse reads as follows:

> "You will hear of wars and rumors of wars, but see to it that you are not alarmed. Such things must happen, but the end is still to come. Nation will rise against nation, and kingdom against kingdom. There will be famines and

earthquakes in various places." (Matt. 24:6-7)

Jesus goes on to say a few verses later:

> *"Then will appear the sign of the Son of Man in heaven. And then all the peoples of the earth will mourn when they see the Son of Man coming on the clouds of heaven, with power and great glory. And he will send his angels with a loud trumpet call, and they will gather his elect from the four winds, from one end of the heavens to the other. "Now learn this lesson from the fig tree: As soon as its twigs get tender and its leaves come out, you know that summer is near. Even so, when you see all these things, you know that it is near, right at the door."* (Matt 24:30-33)

So for many Christians, who are always seeking to faithfully interpret the signs of the times, a series of large scale earthquakes can't help but bring to mind Jesus' words.

However, there are a few problems with this approach that often get overlooked, but which should serve as a caution for any of us who might be tempted to interpret God's actions in the world and the timing of Jesus' return and final judgment:

1. Jesus wasn't talking primarily about the end of the world in the Olivet Discourse.

As we'll see in the next chapter, Jesus was talking about the events that would take place within the Disciples' own lifetimes, particularly regarding the destruction of the Temple in Jerusalem in 70 AD. That is, in fact, with what the entire discussion initially begins! Their question to Jesus was when the Temple would be destroyed and that age be brought to completion (when His messianic reign would begin, presumably). Look again at Jesus' words in the Discourse:

> *"Jesus answered: "Watch out that no one deceives you. For many will come in my name, claiming, 'I am the Messiah,' and will deceive many. You will hear of wars and rumors of wars, but see to it that you are not alarmed. Such things must happen, but the end is still to come. Nation will rise against nation, and kingdom against kingdom. There will be famines and earthquakes in various places. <u>All these are the beginning of birth pains. Then you will be handed over to be persecuted and put to death, and you will be hated by all nations because of me.</u>"* (Matt 24:4-9)

Rather than being the sign of the end of the world, the events Jesus describes would be experienced by His first Disciples, who would then be persecuted and put to death because of their witness to Him--which in fact did happen to 11 of the 12 original Apostles!

2. Jesus wasn't talking primarily about events that would happen thousands of years later.

One of the most frequently made mistakes regarding the Olivet Discourse is to read the "you" throughout it as referring to modern-day Christians. But we don't do that with any other parts of the Gospel where Jesus is addressing His Disciples directly...so why do we do it when we get to the Olivet Discourse?? The "you" throughout whom Jesus addresses are "the Disciples"; the ones who would actually live through the events Jesus was describing in vivid, hyperbole-filled, prophetic language (anyone who doubts whether or not Jesus was using hyperbole should check to make sure they still have a right hand and right eye!).

In fact, lest we have any doubt about the timing of the events Jesus is describing, we need look no further than Jesus' own words.

Look again at the passage about seeing signs and knowing the time is near:

> "*Now learn this lesson from the fig tree: As soon as its twigs get tender and its leaves come out, you know that summer is near. Even so, when you see all these things, you know that it is near, right at the door. <u>Truly I tell you, this generation will certainly not pass away until all these things have happened</u>.*" (Matt 24:32-34)

Jesus says point blank that the events He is talking about, regardless of how they are to be interpreted, will happen within the span of that generation--which, interestingly enough, was exactly when the Temple was, in fact, destroyed!

Some have tried to get around the clear time-cap that Jesus places on His prophetic words by suggesting that "this generation" in v.34 should be translated "this race" (i.e. the Jewish race; cf. the NIV's footnote). However, nowhere else does Jesus use the term in this manner and every time in Matthew when Jesus speaks about "this generation" He is always talking about the generation in which He is living--the generation that witnessed Him in the flesh yet still rejected and put him to death.

Jesus warned of judgment that would come upon that generation many times throughout the Gospels...the Olivet Discourse is simply the final exclamation point and the final prophetic plea by the greatest Prophet in Israel's history for Jerusalem to turn from its rebellion and embrace what God was doing through His Messiah once and for all.

And what's fascinating is that many of them did just that! This is why there were almost no followers of Jesus in Jerusalem when it fell in 70 AD. They understood the signs of the times quite well and fled the city in obedience to Jesus' warning given a generation before!

3. Jesus wasn't talking primarily about His Second Coming.

This is the most common mistake of all that most Christians make when reading the Olivet Discourse. When the Disciples ask Jesus when His "coming" will be, we immediately assume they are asking about His Second Coming (i.e. the Return of Jesus from Heaven to judge the world).

Even many otherwise-excellent study Bibles commit this basic mistake in their notes on this passage. So it's no surprise that the average reader misses this small but crucial detail.

But it is crucial indeed!

When the Disciples ask Jesus about His "coming", they are asking about His "coming [into power]" (i.e. His ascension to the throne of David and His Messianic rule over all the earth). That is what they were expecting.

Remember, the Disciples had no idea that He would be crucified, die, be raised from the dead, ascend to Heaven for thousands of years and then eventually "come" back to earth. Even though He mentioned His impending death numerous times, the Disciples never seem to have accepted that fact (which is why they were so despondent after the events of Good Friday until they saw Him again standing in their midst!)

WE read their question about His "coming" as referring to His Second Coming because we have the benefit of hindsight. But the Disciples were not asking about Jesus' return from Heaven...because they didn't think He would be leaving earth! Again, this is why they were so devasted upon His arrest and crucifixion!

This is also why their belief in His Resurrection was unshakeable after they experienced it--they weren't expecting it to happen or experiencing 'wish-fulfillment' or any of the other psychological phenomena ascribed to them by skeptics.

They were genuinely transformed by their encounter with the Resurrected Jesus!

When Jesus spoke of "*the Son of Man coming*", He was alluding back to the famous "Son of Man" passage in Daniel 7--wherein "*one like a son of man*" comes on the clouds FROM earth TO Heaven to receive universal sovereignty, authority, kingdom and worship from God Almighty.

The "coming" that the Disciples asked about was Jesus' ascension to power and worldwide rule...however, instead of being seated on a throne in Jerusalem, Jesus' ascension was to the Throne of the Universe--"where he sitteth at the right hand of God the Father Almighty", to quote the Apostles' Creed.

Of course, as the Creed goes on to state, "From thence He shall come to judge the quick and the dead"...but the Disciples at the time did not know, nor were they asking about, what we know of as the Second Coming. They were asking about his "coming" to power as Israel's Messiah and the inauguration of the Messianic Age they had been waiting for all their lives.

So why do I say "primarily"??

I've said that Jesus wasn't speaking "primarily" about these things. And I deliberately use that term because of the nature of Hebrew prophecy.

Hebrew prophetic oracles (which is what the Sermon on the Mount most definitely is!) often described events which were to happen on the immediate horizon (i.e. the fall of Babylon, Assyria, Jerusalem, etc.) in language that evokes cosmic, end-of-this-age imagery.

The reason for such imagery and language is likely due to the fact that each time God acts within history as Judge in fulfillment of a prophecy given beforehand, it is a foreshadowing of the *ultimate final Judgment* which will take place on the final "Day of the LORD" (i.e. Judgment Day).

So, in the smaller-scale judgments by God over nations and empires, we get a glimpse of what the final large-scale Judgment of God on all evil once and for all will entail.

This brings us back to the recent earthquakes such as the one in Chile a while back and the recent one in Japan. Are these events "signs of Jesus' return" or "signs of the End"?

No.

At least, not any more so than any natural disaster that has occurred throughout history (ALL of which have been put forth as "signs" by various Christians...all of whom have been wrong thus far!).

The "earthquakes" spoken of by Jesus in the Olivet Discourse happened in the first century (we have record of them throughout the Mediterranean world at that time) and were a sign of the imminent destruction of Jerusalem, the Temple, and the end of that age (i.e. 2nd Temple Judaism).

Ever since then, earthquakes have been happening around the world at a fairly regular rate. With the rise of modern technology and global media, however, we are now able to hear about them much more often, so they seem to have increased in frequency and severity. But in fact, as far as geologists and seismologists tell us, they have not.[9]

HOWEVER...

We do have one instance of Jesus' response to a question about a recent tragic event that happened in Galilee. It's found in Luke's Gospel:

> "Jesus answered, "Do you think that these Galileans were worse sinners than all the other Galileans because they suffered this way? I tell you, no! But unless you repent, you too will all perish. Or those eighteen who died when the tower in Siloam fell on them—do you think they were more guilty than all the others living in Jerusalem? I tell you, no! But unless you repent, you too will all perish." (Luke 13:2-5)

Notice how Jesus turned the question back to His Disciples. When Jesus Himself was asked about disasters and tragic loss of human life, He made it clear that while we cannot always correlate disasters to God's Judgment in a one-to-one manner (i.e. blaming hurricanes in Florida on Disney's celebration of "Gay Day"

[9] See:
http://en.wikipedia.org/wiki/Earthquake#Size_and_frequency_of_oc currence

or Katrina devastating New Orleans on Mardi Gras debauchery...as various Christian media personalities have recklessly done in the past!) we should allow the severity of disasters to remind us that it could've been us who perished in them and whether or not we are ready to face the Final Judgment of a Holy God ourselves.

Of course that's not as "exciting" as trying to read the mind of God into current world events...but it's FAR more important.

And we Christians would do well to do so on a continual basis as we come alongside and support those who suffer and need to see firsthand the Body of Christ in loving action on their behalf .

-Five-
The Temple's Destruction...
From an Eyewitness Account!

During the last week of Jesus' life, when He was teaching in the Temple in Jerusalem, His disciples were awestruck by the Temple's grandeur (as any Galilean peasants and fishermen would've been!).

But Jesus told them that as impressive as it all looked, it would be destroyed brick by brick!

As they left Jerusalem later that afternoon and headed across the valley to the Mt. of Olives, the Disciples asked Jesus to clarify what He had told them. When would the destruction happen and what would be the sign of His coming into power? (As we saw in the last chapter, many readers of the Gospels, upon hearing the Disciples use the word "coming" have mistakenly assumed that they were asking Jesus about His "Second Coming" and thus the end of the world. However, they were asking about His coming to power as Messiah, not His return from Heaven--they didn't even believe that He was going to die at that point, much less ascend to Heaven for a few thousand years and then return afterwards!)

Jesus' answer to their question, which has come to be known as the "Olivet Discourse", can be found in 3 forms in Matthew (24:1-26:2), Mark (13:1-37), and Luke (21:5-38).

This Discourse is given in a format that is very much in keeping with Jesus' role of 1st century apocalyptic prophet. In it, He warns His followers of Jerusalem's coming destruction at the hands of Rome using language and imagery that earlier Hebrew prophets such as Isaiah, Jeremiah, Ezekiel and Daniel used to warn God's people of impending destruction and judgment at the hands of foreign oppressors.

What is especially interesting is that Jesus tells His Disciples that it would all happen within "*this generation*" (Luke 21:32 and parallels). In Scripture, a "generation" is somewhat of a generic unit of time which can be equivalent to roughly 40 years, give or take.

Jesus spoke these words around 30-33 AD. Jerusalem was destroyed in 70 AD...right on schedule.

This has led many scholars who deny the possibility of predictive prophecy altogether, to suggest that the Olivet Discourse is an account composed after the fact and placed on the lips of Jesus in order to validate Him in the eyes of the faithful.

Others, mistaking His description of Jerusalem's fall for a description of the actual end of the world, have taken one of two approaches:

> 1) Jesus was describing the end of the world as taking place within that generation; and since it didn't happen, Jesus was simply wrong.

> 2) Jesus was describing the end of the world, but the phrase "*this generation*" should be translated "*this race*" (i.e. the Jews) or must refer to an unnamed future generation which would exist in Israel at some later date instead. Thus, we are still waiting on the fulfillment of the Olivet Discourse to occur.

However, neither of these approaches seem very acceptable from the perspective of the New Testament as a whole. The first view errs in not recognizing Jesus' use of apocalyptic imagery to describe *the fall of Jerusalem* rather than the end of the world.

The second not only commits that same error, but also insists on translating the word that means "generation" every other time it's used by Jesus as "race" in order to keep Jesus from being wrong in His timetable for the events He's describing. But in context, telling His Disciples that the Jewish people will not pass away until the world ends doesn't make any sense given the question they are asking and the events He is describing.

No, I believe it's much more likely that Jesus is describing the impending judgment by God upon His city and His Temple due to their rejection of God's faithful messenger...who also happens to be their long-awaited Messiah!

Just as Jeremiah had done, Jesus weeps over Jerusalem for its hard-hearted disobedience as a whole (though just as in Jeremiah's day, there is a large remnant of faithful Jews who would survive the destruction and continue bearing the promises of the People of God).

So when we read Jesus' words in the Olivet Discourse we find a *prophetic-apocalyptic* depiction of the destruction of Jerusalem. The use of cosmic imagery and hyperbolic statements are a staple of both the apocalyptic and prophetic genres found throughout Scripture. To press for literalism in the details is to misread the text at a fundamental level. (It would be akin to reading a political cartoon in today's newspaper and then arguing that America was really run by a white-haired man in a stars-and-stripes top hat...or an elephant and donkey who were always fighting!)

But if the events described in the Olivet Discourse are not described using literal language, what did the events themselves actually look like when they occurred?

Is there any way for us to fast forward those 40 years and see it all take place?

Yes, there is.

The Jewish historian, Flavius Josephus, was an eyewitness to the destruction of Jerusalem and wrote about it extensively and in great detail in his historical work "The Jewish Wars." And when we read his account of the events of 70 AD, it gives us a whole new level of appreciation for Jesus' warning to His followers to be on the lookout for such events and to flee the city before they were caught up in them.

It is to Josephus's account that we will now turn.

Here are excerpts from Josephus' *Jewish War* 6:1-406 along with relevant excerpts from the Olivet Discourse as found in Matthew 24:1-51

in bold so that the reader can compare the two.

Josephus on the Destruction of Jerusalem

Thus did the miseries of Jerusalem grow worse and worse every day, and the seditious were still more irritated by the calamities they were under, even while the famine preyed upon themselves, after it had preyed upon the people. And, indeed, the multitude of carcasses that lay in heaps one upon another was a horrible sight, and produced a pestilential stench, which was a hindrance to those who would make sallies out of the city and fight the enemy... but as they had their right hands already polluted with the murders of their own countrymen,

"At that time many will turn away from the faith and will betray and hate each other..." (Matthew 24:10)

and in that condition ran out to fight with foreigners, they seem to me to have cast a reproach upon God himself, as if he were too slow in punishing them... And truly, the very view itself of the country was a melancholy thing; for those places which were before adorned with trees and pleasant gardens, were now become a desolate country all over, and its trees were all cut down: nor could any foreigner that had formerly seen Judea and the most beautiful suburbs of the city, and now saw it as a desert, but lament and mourn sadly at so great a change; for the war had laid all the signs of beauty quite waste: nor, if anyone that had known the place before had come suddenly to it now, would he have known it again...

"Jesus left the temple and was walking away when his disciples came up to him to call his attention to its buildings. 2 "Do you see all these things?" he asked. "I tell you the truth, not one stone here will be left on another; every one will be thrown down." (Matthew 24:1)

Josephus on the Famine in the City

Now of those who perished by famine in the city, the number was prodigious, and the miseries they underwent were unspeakable; for if so much as the shadow of any kind of food did anywhere appear, a war was commenced immediately, and the dearest friends started fighting one with another about it, snatching from each other the most miserable supports of life. Nor would men believe that those who were dying had no food; but the robbers would search them when they were expiring, lest anyone should have concealed food in their bosoms, and counterfeited dying: nay, these robbers gaped for want, and ran about stumbling and staggering along like mad dogs, and reeling against the doors of the houses like drunken men; they would also, in the great distress they were in, rush into the very same houses two or three times in one and the same day. Moreover, their hunger was so intolerable, that it obliged them to chew everything, while they gathered such things as the most sordid animals would not touch, and endured to eat them; nor did they at length abstain from belts and shoes; and the very leather which belonged to their shields they pulled off and gnawed: the very wisps of old hay became food to some; and some gathered up fibers, and sold a very small weight of them for four Attic [drachmas].

"You will hear of wars and rumors of wars, but see to it that you are not alarmed. Such things must happen, but the end is still to come. Nation will rise against nation, and kingdom against kingdom. There will be famines and earthquakes in various places. All these are the beginning of birth pains." (Matthew 24:6-8)

But why do I describe the shameless impudence that the famine brought on men in their eating inanimate things, while I am going to relate a matter of fact, the like to which no history relates, either among the Greeks or Barbarians?

It is horrible to speak of it, and incredible when heard.

Josephus on Jerusalem Under Siege and Resorting to Cannibalism

There was a certain woman that dwelt beyond Jordan--her name was Mary...[she] was with them besieged therein at this time...what food she had contrived to save, had been also carried off by the rapacious guards, who came every day running into her house for that purpose... if she found any food, she perceived her labors were for others, and not for herself; and it was now...impossible for...to find any more food, while the famine pierced through her very bowels and marrow... She then attempted a most unnatural thing; and snatching up her son, who was a child sucking at her breast, she said, ``O you miserable infant! for whom shall I preserve you in this war, this famine, and this sedition? As to the war with the Romans, if they preserve our lives, we must be slaves! This famine also will kill us, even before that slavery comes upon us; yet are these seditious rogues more terrible than both of the other. Come on; be my food, and be a fury to these seditious rebels...."

As soon as she had said this, she slew her son; and then roasted him, and eat the one half of him, and kept the other half by her concealed.

Upon this the [rebels] came in presently, and smelling the horrid scent of this food, they threatened her that they would cut her throat immediately if she did not show them what food she had gotten ready. She replied, that she had saved a very fine portion of it for them; and with this uncovered what was left of her son.

Hereupon they were seized with a horror and amazement of mind, and stood astonished at the sight; when she said to them, ``This is my own son, and what has been done was my own doing! Come, eat of this food; for I have eaten of it myself!"

...the whole city was [told] of this horrid action immediately; and while everyone laid this miserable case before their own eyes, they trembled, as if this unheard of action had been done by themselves. So those that were thus distressed by the famine were very desirous to die; and those already dead were esteemed happy, because they had not lived long enough either to hear or to see such miseries.

"How dreadful it will be in those days for pregnant women and nursing mothers! Pray that your flight will not take place in winter or on the Sabbath. For then there will be great distress, unequaled from the beginning of the world until now-- and never to be equaled again." (Matthew 24:19-21)

Josephus on the Temple Fire

...While the holy house was on fire, everything was plundered that came to hand, and ten thousand of those who were caught were slain; nor was there a pity of any age, or any reverence of gravity; but children, and old men, and common persons, and priests were all slain in the same manner; so that this war went around all sorts of men, and brought them to destruction, and as well those who made supplication for their lives, as those who defended themselves by fighting.

"So when you see standing in the holy place 'the abomination that causes desolation,' spoken of through the prophet Daniel-- let the reader understand--then let those who are in Judea flee to the mountains. (Matthew 24:15-16)

The flame was also carried a long way, and made an echo, together with the groans of those who were slain; and because this hill was high, and the works at the temple were very large, one would have thought the whole city had been on fire. Nor can one imagine anything either greater or more terrible than this noise... for the ground did nowhere appear visible, for the dead bodies that lay on it; but the soldiers went over heaps of those bodies, as they ran upon such as fled from them...

"Wherever there is a carcass, there the vultures/eagles will gather." (Matthew 24:28)

Josephus on False Prophets and Foreboding Signs

A false prophet was the occasion of these people's destruction, who had made a public proclamation in the city that very day, that God commanded them to get upon the temple, and that there they should receive miraculous signs of their deliverance. Now there was then a great number of false prophets bribed by the tyrants to impose on the people, who announced this to them, that they should wait for deliverance from God; and this was in order to keep them from deserting, and that they might be buoyed up above fear and care by such hopes. Thus were the miserable people persuaded by these deceivers, and such as belied God himself; while they did not attend nor give credit to the signs that were so evident, and did so plainly foretell their future desolation; but, like men infatuated, without either eyes to see or minds to consider, did not regard the denunciations that God made to them.

Jesus answered: "Watch out that no one deceives you. For many will come in my name, claiming, 'I am the Christ,' and will deceive many... and many false prophets will appear and deceive many people... At that time if

**anyone says to you, 'Look, here is the Christ!'
or, 'There he is!' do not believe it. For false
Christs and false prophets will appear and
perform great signs and miracles to deceive
even the elect-- if that were possible. See, I
have told you ahead of time."** (Matthew 24:4-
5, 11, 23-25)

*Thus there was a star resembling a sword,
which stood over the city, and a comet, that
continued a whole year... Thus also, before the
Jews' rebellion, and before those commotions
which preceded the war...on the eighth day of
the month of Nisan...and at the ninth hour of
the night, so great a light shone around the
altar and the holy house, that it appeared to be
bright daytime; which lasted for half an hour.
This light seemed to be a good sign to the
unskillful, but was so interpreted by the sacred
scribes as to portend those events that followed
immediately upon it... So these publicly
declared that the signal predicted the
desolation that was coming upon them.*

**"For as lightening that comes from the east is
visible even in the west, so will be the coming
of the Son of Man... Immediately after the
distress of those days "'the sun will be
darkened, and the moon will not give its light;
the stars will fall from the sky, and the
heavenly bodies will be shaken.'** (Matthew
24:27, 29)

66

Besides these, a few days after that feast, on the twenty-first day of the month of Lyyar a certain prodigious and incredible phenomenon appeared: I suppose the account of it would seem to be a fable, were it not related by those who saw it, and were not the events that followed it of so considerable a nature as to deserve such signals; for, before sunset, chariots and troops of soldiers in their armor were seen running about among the clouds, and surrounding the cities.

"At that time the sign of the Son of Man will appear in the sky, and all the nations of the earth will mourn. They will see the Son of Man coming on the clouds of the sky, with power and great glory." (Matthew 24:30)

Moreover, at that feast which we call Pentecost, as the priests were going by night into the inner court of the temple, as their custom was, to perform their sacred ministrations, they said that, in the first place, they felt a quaking, and heard a great noise, and after that they heard a sound as of a great multitude, saying, ``We are departing from here"...

And he will send his angels with a loud trumpet call, and they will gather his elect from the four winds, from one end of the heavens to the other. (Matthew 24:31)

Josephus on the Lament of Jesus, Son of Ananus

...But, what is still more terrible, there was one Jesus, the son of Ananus, a common man and a husbandman, who, four years before the war began, and at a time when the city was in very great peace and prosperity, came to that feast whereon it is our custom for everyone to make tabernacles to God in the temple, began suddenly to cry aloud, ``A voice from the east, a voice from the west, a voice from the four winds, a voice against Jerusalem and the holy house, a voice against the bridegroom and the bride, and a voice against this whole people!"

This was his cry, as he went about by day and by night, in all the lanes of the city. However, certain of the most eminent among the populace had great indignation at this dire cry of his, and took up the man, and gave him a great number of severe stripes; yet he did not either say anything for himself, or anything peculiar to those who chastised him, but still went on with the same words which he cried before.

Hereupon our rulers supposing, as the case proved to be, that this was a sort of divine fury in the man, brought him to the Roman procurator; where he was whipped till his bones were laid bare; yet he did not make any *supplication for himself, nor shed any tears, but turning his voice to the most lamentable tone possible, at every stroke of the whip his answer was, ``Woe, woe to Jerusalem!''...*

Then you will be handed over to be persecuted and put to death, and you will be hated by all nations because of me. (Matthew 24:9)

Now, during all the time that passed before the war began, this man did not go near anyone of the citizens, nor was seen by them while he said so; but he every day uttered these lamentable words, as if it were his premeditated vow, ``Woe, woe to Jerusalem!''

Nor did he give ill words to any of those who beat him every day, nor good words to those who gave him food; but this was his reply to all men, and indeed no other than a melancholy presage of what was to come.

This cry of his was the loudest at the festivals; and he continued this dirge for seven years and five months, without growing hoarse, or being tired therewith, until the very time that he saw his presage in earnest fulfilled in our siege, when it ceased; for as he was going around upon the wall, he cried out with his utmost force, ``Woe, woe to the city again, and to the people, and to the holy house!'' And just as he added at the last, ``Woe, woe to myself also!''

there came a stone out of one of the engines, and smote him, and killed him immediately; and as he was uttering the very same presages he gave up the ghost.

Now learn this lesson from the fig tree: As soon as its twigs get tender and its leaves come out, you know that summer is near. Even so, when you see all these things, you know that it is near, right at the door. I tell you the truth, this generation will certainly not pass away until all these things have happened. Heaven and earth will pass away, but my words will never pass away. (Matthew 24:32-35)

Josephus on the Massive Slaughter Within the City

But when [the Roman soldiers] went in numbers into the lanes of the city with their swords drawn, they slew those whom they overtook without mercy, and set fire to the houses where the Jews were fled, and burnt every soul in them, and laid waste a great many of the rest;

As it was in the days of Noah, so it will be at the coming of the Son of Man. For in the days before the flood, people were eating and drinking, marrying and giving in marriage, up to the day Noah entered the ark; and they knew nothing about what would happen until

the flood came and took them all away. That is how it will be at the coming of the Son of Man. Two men will be in the field; one will be taken and the other left. Two women will be grinding with a hand mill; one will be taken and the other left. "Therefore keep watch, because you do not know on what day your Lord will come. (Matthew 24:37-42)

and when they were come to the houses to plunder them, they found in them entire families of dead men, and the upper rooms full of dead corpses, that is, of such as died by the famine; they then stood in a horror at this sight, and went out without touching anything. But although they had this pity for such as were killed in that manner, yet had they not the same for those who were still alive, but they ran everyone through whom they met with, and obstructed the very lanes with their dead bodies, and made the whole city run down with blood, to such a degree indeed, that the fire of many of the houses was quenched with these men's blood.

Let no one on the roof of his house go down to take anything out of the house. Let no one in the field go back to get his cloak. (Matthew 24:17)

So when we read the account of Jerusalem's destruction, and then go back and reread the Olivet Discourse, we see that Jesus was the last in a long line of Prophets who warned Jerusalem of impending judgment and destruction at the hands of pagan oppressors.

Through the use of apocalyptic imagery and prophetic hyperbole, just as Jeremiah, Ezekiel, Isaiah and Daniel had done centuries before Him, Jesus foretold this earth-shattering event in such a way that when the events actually happened, those who had heard His words and taken them to heart had already fled the city and had begun to take the message of their Messiah to all corners of the Roman Empire.

And seeing the Olivet Discourse through the eyes of its horribly, bloody, historical aftermath reveals why Jesus was so distraught and intent on getting His Disciples to realize the gravity of what was on the horizon.

However, as we noted in the last chapter, like almost all Biblical prophecy, the events foretold in the Olivet Discourse are also paradigmatic of the final "Day of the LORD" and thus point beyond the events surrounding 70 AD to the culmination of God's judgment and the final "coming of the Son of Man in power."

Thus, while Jesus' words in Matthew 24 refer primarily to the events surrounding 70 AD and the end of the age of the Jerusalem Temple, they may also give us a glimpse of what it will be like on a cosmic scale at the end of the current age when God judges evil once and for all through His returning, reigning Messiah and Son.

-Six-
Reading Revelation
On Its Own Terms

Revelation is widely-believed to be the most mysterious and scary book in the Bible. This is unfortunate because for the early Christians, Revelation was the most *comforting* and helped make things *clearer* to them regarding what they were living through and how it all fit in with God's overall plan of redemptive history.

Therefore, it should be studied by Christians today, not in order to chart out various end-times scenarios or decide which world leader is which beastly creature in the book[10], but rather to hear the voice of Jesus to His people throughout the ages, including His people today.

First things, first...it's the book of "*Revelation*"—not "*Revelations.*"

Whenever you hear someone say, "well, you know what it says in Revelations..." you ought to be a bit skeptical of their authority to teach a book whose actual title eludes them.

---

[10] for a somewhat surreal example of such an approach--set to song, no less!—visit: http://jmsmith.org/blog/warning-awful-folk-theology-meets-awful-folk-music/

Revelation.

No "s" involved!

Now that we have that out of the way, let's talk about the word itself. "Revelation" is the Greek word "*apocalupsis*" which means "unveiling" or "revealing" (thus "revelation") and it is the very first word in the book:

> *"The revelation of Jesus the Messiah..."* (1:1a)

One of the most amazing (and saddest) ironies in the history of Bible study is that the very book written to make things clear is actually one of the most misunderstood, intimidating and divisive books in the entire Bible!

Now while some of this is due to sinful divisiveness or pride in interpreting, much of it is due simply to a lack of awareness not only of the book's historical context, but also a general unfamiliarity with the Hebrew Bible and Second-Temple Jewish literature from which the imagery of Revelation draws extensively. Any reading of Revelation that does not take these into account will almost certainly veer off course and be far from what the Holy Spirit intended to teach through John's apocalyptic vision.

So what exactly did Jesus want to "unveil" to John and his fellow 1st century Christians? And why did He choose an apocalyptic vision as the vehicle for conveying it? And, just as important, what does Revelation have to do with Christians today who are millennia removed from the time it in which it was written?

Is it an outdated book meant only for 1st century Christians?

Is it a blueprint of end-times events which we are currently seeing play out in the news every day?

Or is it something completely different?

While we can't cover the answers to these questions in exhaustive detail, (though these and other questions *are* more fully explored in Disciple Dojo's "Revelation: A Guided Tour of the Apocalypse" DVD study, from which this chapter is adapted[11]) the following are a few helpful details to know when studying Revelation:

1. Revelation is believed to have been written during the reign of the Roman Emperor Domitian around 90 AD (though some notable

---

[11] http://jmsmith.org/store/revelation/

Biblical scholars have proposed a date sometime in the 60s AD before the destruction of the Jerusalem Temple (70 AD) and during the reign of the Emperor Nero). Those dating it to Domitian see the references to Nero in Revelation (of which there are quite a few) as being symbolic of *all* subsequent persecuting rulers, such as Domitian, who would arise in the manner of Nero. Those who date it to Nero's time see it as predicting the persecution that is about to take place (or is currently taking place) at the hands of the Roman Empire under his terrible reign. Either view, however, ultimately arrives at the same overall conclusion as to the meaning and message of the book.

2. Revelation belongs to the Biblical genre of "*Apocalyptic*". Apocalyptic writings date as far back as the OT prophets Daniel and Zechariah, and were extremely popular during the 1st few centuries BC and up through around the 2nd century AD. Apocalyptic writings usually consist of visions (and sometimes interpretations of them) given to a human recipient by a heavenly messenger which seek to provide clarity, encouragement, and comfort to a persecuted minority at the hands of an oppressive ruling majority.

Apocalypses were never intended to only communicate events that would happen at the end of time; but rather, they were written to communicate current or imminent events that the community or nation was about to experience or was experiencing already. *Ignoring the genre of the book is one of the biggest mistakes many readers—especially many so-called "prophecy experts"—make when interpreting and teaching Revelation.* This often (though in fairness, not always) results in wild scenarios of raptures, credit card chip implants and even protests against peace attempts in areas of the world they see as having "end times significance"! (All three of these, for example, have been taught by extremely prominent Evangelical Christian leaders in the public eye within the last 20 years. This is beyond unfortunate...it's irresponsible).

3. It was not uncommon for Roman Emperors such as Nero or Domitian to declare themselves Divine and adopt titles such as "Lord", "Savior", or "Son of God"...or even demand worship on threat of death.

4. Apocalyptic literature was *never* meant to be read purely "literally." This is worth repeating because an entire segment of Evangelical Christianity beginning in the 1850s began to insist that the literal meaning of Biblical text was the only valid meaning...unless of course it was absolutely impossible to read it literally (such as Jesus being called a "Lamb"). This was an extremely ill-informed conclusion on the part of those who did not know that the nature of Apocalyptic writing is *primarily non-literal and highly symbolic.*

However, due to the popularity of many Christian teachers and pastors who hold to this method of interpretation, the "literal" reading of Revelation (and other Biblical apocalyptic texts) became the default approach among many Evangelical Christians. To this day, there are various Bible colleges and Seminaries which accept only the "literal" interpretation of Revelation and many otherwise solid Christian leaders and teachers have adopted and continue to perpetuate this approach.

5. Apocalyptic literature uses certain well-known symbols and metaphors, often drawn from the Hebrew Bible, to convey ideas, traits or circumstances in a vivid visionary manner. Some examples of these are:

- Trees
- trumpets
- menorahs (lampstands)
- horns
- numbers
- books/scrolls and their seals

- the Sea/Abyss
- cosmic bodies (Sun, Moon, stars)
- "Israel"
- "Egypt"
- "Babylon"
- jewels and precious stones and metals
- plagues
- thunder, lighting and earthquakes (theophany)

There are many others but these are some of the most frequently occurring ones found in Revelation.

6. Revelation was meant to be read aloud during worship gatherings among the early churches throughout Asia Minor. It was sometimes read all the way through, and sometimes divided into multiple sections and read aloud by a leader in the church. Thus, there is great importance in *listening* to Revelation rather than merely reading it silently. It's also why churches should include it in their liturgical readings rather than ignoring it because it is "weird."

Recommended Resources for Studying Revelation

General Overviews:

- Bauckham, Richard. The Climax of Prophecy. T&T Clark, New York. 1993.
- Bauckham, Richard. The Theology of the Book of Revelation. Cambridge, Cambridge. 2002
- Gundry, Stanley N., ed. Four Views on the Book of Revelation. Zondervan, Grand Rapids. 1998.
- Koester, Craig. Revelation and the End of All Things. Eerdmans, Grand Rapids. 2001.
- Lowry, Robert. Revelation's Rhapsody: Listening to the Lyrics of the Lamb. College Press Publishing Co. 2006.
- Spilsbury, Paul. The Throne, the Lamb & the Dragon: A Reader's Guide to the Book of Revelation. InterVarsity, Downers Grove. 2002
- Wilson, Mark. Charts on the Book of Revelation: Literary, Historical, and Theological Perspectives. Kregel, Grand Rapids. 2007.

Non-technical Commentaries:

- Barclay, William. <u>The Revelation of John, 2 vols</u>. Westminster, Philadelphia. 1960
- Boring, Eugene M. <u>Revelation: Interpretation</u>. John Knox, Louisville. 1989.
- Boxall, Ian. <u>The Revelation of Saint John: Black's New Testament Commentary</u>. Hendrickson, Peabody. 2006.
- Caird, G.B. <u>The Revelation of Saint John: Black's New Testament Commentary</u>. Hendrickson, Peabody. 1999.
- Gregg, Steve, ed. <u>Revelation - Four Views: A Parallel Commentary</u>. Thomas Nelson, Nashville. 1997.
- Keener, Craig S. <u>Revelation: The NIV Application Commentary</u>. Zondervan, Grand Rapids. 2000.
- Osborne, Grant R. <u>Revelation: Baker Exegetical Commentary on the New Testament</u>. Baker, Grand Rapids. 2002.
- Witherington, Ben. <u>Revelation: The New Cambridge Bible Commentary</u>. Cambridge, New York. 2003.

Technical Commentaries:

- Aune, David E. <u>Revelation: Word Biblical Commentary, 3 vols</u>. Thomas Nelson, Nashville. 1998.
- Beale, G.K. <u>The New International Greek Testament Commentary: Revelation</u>. Eerdmans, Grand Rapids. 1999.
- Beale, G.K. and Carson, D.A. <u>Commentary on the New Testament Use of the Old Testament</u>. Baker, Grand Rapids. 2007.
- Mounce, Robert H. <u>The Book of Revelation: The New International Commentary on the New Testament</u>. Eerdmans, Grand Rapids. 1977.

Other Jewish Apocalyptic Writings[12]

"*Book of the Watchers*" (1 Enoch 1-36) – 3rd Century BC

"*Book of the Heavenly Luminaries*" (1 Enoch 73-82) – 3rd Century BC

"*Animal Apocalypse*" (1 Enoch 85-90) – 2nd Century BC

"*Apocalypse of Weeks*" (1 Enoch 91:11-17; 93:1-10) – 2nd Century BC

Jubilees 23 – 2nd Century BC

---

[12] [Wilson, *Charts on the Book of Revelation*]

Testament of Levi 2-5 – 2nd Century BC
Testament of Abraham – 1st Century BC-
2nd Century AD
Apocalypse of Zephaniah – 1st Century
BC-1st Century AD
"*Similitudes of Enoch*" (1 Enoch 37-71)
– 1st Century AD
2 Enoch – 1st Century AD
4 Ezra – 1st Century AD
2 Baruch – 1st Century AD
Apocalpyse of Abraham – 1st-2nd
Century AD
3 Baruch – 1st-2nd Century AD

Other Christian Apocalyptic Writings

Shepherd of Hermas – 1st-2nd Century
AD
Book of Elchasai – 1st-2nd Century AD
Ascension of Isaiah 6-11 – 1st-2nd
Century AD
Apocalypse of Peter – 2nd Century AD
5 Ezra 2:42-48 – 2nd – 3rd Century AD?
Jacob's Ladder – 2nd Century AD?
Testament of the Lord 1:1-14 – 3rd
Century AD?
Apocalypse of Sedrach – 2nd-4th
Century AD?
Apocalypse of Paul – 4th Century AD?
Testament of Isaac – 1st-5th Century AD?

Testament of Jacob – 2nd – 5th Century AD?
Story of Zosimus – 3rd-5th Century AD?
Apocalypse of St. John the Theologian – 2nd-9th Century AD?

Genres Found in Revelation

Apocalyptic
Prophecy
Epistle

Proposed Structures of Revelation

Threefold based on 1:19

I.   What you have seen (1:1-20)
II.   What is now (2:1-3:21)
III. What will take place later (4:1-22:21)

Fourfold based on "In the Spirit"

I.   In the Spirit on the Island of Patmos (1:9-10)
II.   In the Spirit in Heaven (4:1-2)
III. In the Spirit in the Desert (17:3)
IV.   In the Spirit on a Mountain (21:10)

Sevenfold Drama

Prologue (1:1-8)
Act 1 – The 7 Golden Menorahs (1:9-3:22)
Act 2 – The 7 Seals (4:1-8:4)
Act 3 – The 7 Trumpets (8:5-11:18)
Act 4 – The 7 Tableaux (11:19-15:4)
Act 5 – The 7 Bowls/Cups (15:5-16:21) [or (15:5-19:10)]
Act 6 – The 7 Judgments (17:1-20:3) [or 7 Final Visions (19:11-22:11)]
Act 7 – The 7 Promises (20:4-22:5)
Epilogue (22:6-21)

Chiastic

A – Prologue & Greeting (1:1-8)
 B – 7 Churches (1:4-4:2)
  C – 7 Seals (3:21-8:5)
   D – 7 Trumpets/Angels/2 Witnesses (8:2-11:19)
    E – Woman/Dragon/Male Child (12:1-17)

   D' – 2 Beasts/Angels/7 Bowls (13:1-16:21
  C' – Destruction of Babylon (16:18-19:10)
 B' – New Jerusalem/Bride (19:6-22:9)
A' – Closing & Epilogue (22:6-21)

Some Thoughts on Revelation by noted scholars:

"*For those who were tired of being pushed around by the Romans and who may have been in danger of being disillusioned as believers, John wants to assure them that what they see happening is only part of the picture. God has a purpose that he is working out in history, which will result in the reign of God over every principality and prince in the world.*"

–Walter C. Kaiser

"*What the book of Revelation does, in keeping with its apocalyptic genre, is to life the curtain which hides the unseen world of spiritual reality and to show us what is going on behind the scenes...*

This age-long battle is set forth in a series of dramatic visions which have been variously interpreted as depicting the historical development at that time (the 'preterist' school), through the succeeding centuries (the 'historicist' school) or as a prelude to the End (the 'futurist'). None of these is altogether satisfactory, however. The visions cannot portray successive events in a continuous sequence, since the final judgment and victory are dramatized several times. It seems more probably, therefore, that the scenes overlap;

that the whole history of the world between Christ's first coming (the victory won) and second (the victory conceded) is several time recapitulated in vision; and that the emphasis is on the conflict between the Lamb and the dragon which has already had a number of historical manifestations, and will have more before the End.

The message of the book of Revelation is that Jesus Christ has defeated Satan and will one day destroy him altogether. It is in the light of these certainties that we are to confront his continuing malicious activity, whether physical (through persecution), intellectual (through deception) or moral (through corruption)."

– John R.W. Stott

"The Book of Revelation is not about predicting the future in great detail but rather it is about how disciples of Jesus are to live in light of a future that belongs to God."

– Robert Lowery

-Seven-
A Friendly Discussion About

End-Time Assumptions

When it comes to the popular understanding of "End Times" teachings of the Bible (which most often reflect a 19th century form of Biblical interpretation known as *Dispensationalism*), many Christians have a particular lens through which they have been taught to read Scripture.

In fact, beginning with the famous Scofield Reference Bible at the beginning of the 1900s, many Bible publishers have put forth different study Bibles containing all manner of theological views which are put in the margins or at the bottom of the page, to which readers can refer for guidance when reading difficult passages.

This is not necessarily a bad thing!

But it can often lead readers to unconsciously, or semi-consciously, adopt the view of their favorite study Bible's particular theological approach.

It's important, therefore, to have our underlying assumptions continuously challenged. And when it comes to Dispensational assumptions about Scripture's teachings on the "End Times", there are many such assumptions that are worth ferreting out in discussion.

The following are excerpts from a discussion I once had with a good friend (and dear brother in Christ) about some of these very things. He subscribes to the standard Dispensational view of the End Times known as "Pre-Trib" (short for Pre-Tribulation, which refers to a subset of Dispensationalism. Pre-Trib proponents generally follow the "Left Behind" script and believe Jesus will rapture the Church out of the world before the "Great Tribulation"...thus the term "Pre-Trib").[13] My response to comments my friend made in our discussion of a number of points are in **bold** below:

I. On Jesus' words in Matthew 24-25

Pre-Trib Friend: *I believe Jesus was referring to the generation that would not only see the signs, but most importantly, experience the*

---

[13] For a fuller overview of the various End Times positions Christians have held along with an in-depth look at Dispensationalism, see the "Apocalypse Now??" CD course in the Disciple Dojo resource store (http://jmsmith.org/store) or podcast link at the top of the Disciple Dojo homepage (http://jmsmith.org).

"birth pains". The birth pains He mentioned to me indicates that all the wars, famines, plagues, natural disasters etc. are going to get progressively worse and on a more epic scale, just as the pains of birth get worse and more frequent.

JM: This is the only way that the Pre-trib view can work. Unfortunately, the discourse is pretty clear in multiple ways that Jesus is speaking to His disciples about their own current generation--just as He had when He spoke elsewhere in Matthew about "this generation":

"To what can I compare <u>this generation</u>? They are like children sitting in the marketplaces and calling out to others: "'We played the flute for you, and you did not dance; we sang a dirge, and you did not mourn.' For John came neither eating nor drinking, and they say, 'He has a demon.' The Son of Man came eating and drinking, and they say, 'Here is a glutton and a drunkard, a friend of tax collectors and "sinners."' 'But wisdom is proved right by her actions." (Matthew 11:16-19)

He answered, "A <u>wicked and adulterous generation</u> asks for a miraculous sign! But none will be given it except the

sign of the prophet Jonah. For as Jonah
was three days and three nights in the
belly of a huge fish, so the Son of Man
will be three days and three nights in
the heart of the earth. The men of
Nineveh will stand up at the judgment
with this generation and condemn it;
for they repented at the preaching of
Jonah, and now one greater than Jonah
is here. The Queen of the South will rise
at the judgment with this generation
and condemn it; for she came from the
ends of the earth to listen to Solomon's
wisdom, and now one greater than
Solomon is here. "When an evil spirit
comes out of a man, it goes through
arid places seeking rest and does not
find it. Then it says, 'I will return to the
house I left.' When it arrives, it finds the
house unoccupied, swept clean and put
in order. Then it goes and takes with it
seven other spirits more wicked than
itself, and they go in and live there. And
the final condition of that man is worse
than the first. That is how it will be with
this wicked generation." (Matthew
12:39-45)

A wicked and adulterous generation
looks for a miraculous sign, but none
will be given it except the sign of

Jonah." Jesus then left them and went away. (Matthew 16:4)

"O unbelieving and perverse generation," Jesus replied, "how long shall I stay with you? How long shall I put up with you? Bring the boy here to me." Jesus rebuked the demon, and it came out of the boy, and he was healed from that moment. (Matthew 17:17-18)

Therefore I am sending you prophets and wise men and teachers. Some of them you will kill and crucify; others you will flog in your synagogues and pursue from town to town. And so upon you will come all the righteous blood that has been shed on earth, from the blood of righteous Abel to the blood of Zechariah son of Berekiah, whom you murdered between the temple and the altar. I tell you the truth, all this will come upon this generation. (Matthew 23:34-36)

The generation being spoken of is definitely Jesus' contemporary generation. Now look at His words regarding the destruction of the Temple and Jerusalem which many have mistakenly interpreted as a primarily a prediction of a Pre-trib Rapture scenario:

Matthew 24:1 Jesus left <u>the temple</u> and was walking away when his disciples came up to him <u>to call his attention to its buildings</u>.

2 "Do you see all these things?" he asked. "I tell you the truth, not one stone here will be left on another; every one will be thrown down."

3 As Jesus was sitting on the Mount of Olives, the disciples came to him privately. "Tell us," they said, "<u>when will this happen, and what will be the sign of your coming and of the end of the age</u>?"

4 Jesus answered: "Watch out that no one deceives <u>you</u>. 5 For many will come in my name, claiming, 'I am the Christ,' and will deceive many. 6 You will hear of wars and rumors of wars, but see to it that <u>you</u> are not alarmed. Such things must happen, <u>but the end is still to come</u>. 7 Nation will rise against nation, and kingdom against kingdom. There will be famines and earthquakes in various places. 8 All these are <u>the beginning of birth pains</u>.

9 "Then <u>you</u> will be handed over to be persecuted and put to death, and you will be hated by all nations because of me. 10 <u>At that time</u> many will turn away from the faith and will betray and hate each other, 11 and

many false prophets will appear and deceive many people. 12 Because of the increase of wickedness, the love of most will grow cold, 13 but he who stands firm to the end will be saved.

14 And this gospel of the kingdom will be preached in the whole world as a testimony to all nations, and then the end will come.

15 "So when you see standing in the holy place 'the abomination that causes desolation,' spoken of through the prophet Daniel-- let the reader understand-- 16 then let those who are in Judea flee to the mountains. 17 Let no one on the roof of his house go down to take anything out of the house. 18 Let no one in the field go back to get his cloak. 19 How dreadful it will be in those days for pregnant women and nursing mothers! 20 Pray that your flight will not take place in winter or on the Sabbath. 21 For then there will be great distress, unequaled from the beginning of the world until now--and never to be equaled again. 22 If those days had not been cut short, no one would survive, but for the sake of the elect those days will be shortened.

23 At that time if anyone says to you, 'Look, here is the Christ!' or, 'There he is!' do not believe it. 24 For false

Christs and false prophets will appear and perform great signs and miracles to deceive even the elect--if that were possible. 25 See, <u>I have told you</u> ahead of time. 26 "So if anyone tells <u>you</u>, 'There he is, out in the desert,' do not go out; or, 'Here he is, in the inner rooms,' do not believe it. 27 <u>For as lightning that comes from the east is visible even in the west, so will be the coming of the Son of Man</u>. 28 Wherever there is a carcass, there the vultures will gather.

29 "Immediately after the distress of <u>those days</u> "'the sun will be darkened, and the moon will not give its light; the stars will fall from the sky, and the heavenly bodies will be shaken.' 30 "At that time <u>the sign of the Son of Man</u> will appear in the sky, and all the nations of the earth will mourn. They will see <u>the Son of Man coming on the clouds of Heaven</u>, with power and great glory. 31 And he will send his angels/messengers with a loud trumpet call, and they will gather his elect from the four winds, from one end of the heavens to the other.

32 "Now learn this lesson from the fig tree: As soon as its twigs get tender and its leaves come out, you know that summer is near. 33 Even so, when <u>you</u>

see all these things, you know that it is near, right at the door. 34 I tell you the truth, this generation will certainly not pass away until all these things have happened. 35 Heaven and earth will pass away, but my words will never pass away.

In good Jewish, Prophetic, Apocalyptic fashion, Jesus takes their questions about the end of their age and His teaching about the destruction of Jerusalem and uses it to describe the events that will accompany it. And while this certainly does function as a prophetic "type" of the ultimate final coming in Judgment at the end of history, the primary emphasis is on Jesus' own generation--the 40 years between His death and the fall of Jerusalem in 70 A.D.

To read all of this as describing only a future time of suffering (and add in a notion of a 'rapture') is simply not grammatically or contextually plausible. One must *first* arrive at a Pre-trib Rapture theology, as John Nelson Darby did in the 1850s and then read this passage (and its parallels in the other synoptic Gospels) through the lens of that system. But this is *reading into Scripture* rather than interpreting its original meaning.

II. On current world events resembling Jesus' words

Pre-Trib Friend: *But you have to admit that with the weapons and technology we have today that the stakes have increased exponentially. We now have the ability to exterminate everyone in the world, or control them through technology (cybernetic implants, tracking devices, etc.). Look around at how weather patterns have changed, how hurricanes are so much worse, how much of the earth is turning to desert. Look at the famines and diseases like AIDS that ravage the world. Look at the anti-Christian activism all over the world. In Europe, once the most zealous continent, less than 5% of the population even attends church now. Islam/terrorism is spreading. Everything the Pre-Trib Dispensational crowd has been predicting for years is happening today. The world is turning more and more against God each day. How long will He allow it to go on?*

JM: While this description of the world seems accurate from our perspective, this exact argument has been used by *every single generation* since the middle ages as evidence that they were near the end of things. In other words, there has never been since Jesus when the world was not going through famines, droughts, earthquakes, wars, disease (black plague?), and other massive suffering.

But if we read Jesus' words as Apocalyptic descriptions of the fall of Jerusalem and the destruction of the Temple (He employs OT imagery describing the destruction of various nations hundreds of years before), then we won't make the mistake that every successive generation has made in trying to fit current events to these particular images.

Pre-Trib Friend: *Ah yes, but the descriptions of how things will be in the Tribulation are completely different from history up to that time.*

Mark 13:19 - "because those will be days of distress unequaled from the beginning, when God created the world, until now and never to be equaled again."

The wars, persecution, etc. of history have been horrible, but the Tribulation will be Satan's final attempt to wipe all trace of God from the earth.

JM: If Jesus had never spoken in hyperbole, then I could concede this point to you. However, Jesus frequent use of hyperbole, combined with the already Apocalyptic nature of the imagery being used (stars falling from the sky, etc.), combined with the amazing atrocities that Josephus reports as having taken place during the seige in 70 A.D., makes it seem much more probable that Jesus is primarily referring to the period between 30-70A.D.--*which may possibly foreshadow* the future time right up until His actual return at the End of the Age.

III. On Jesus prediction of some being "left behind."

Pre-Trib Disp: *Just like God saved Noah and his family from the wrath that He unleashed upon the rest of the world, so God will Rapture Christians out of the world before the Tribulation. Noah suffered before he entered the ark, but God spared him from the final judgment that the wicked endured. I think it would be against God's love to indiscriminately wipe out all his followers along with the rest of the world.*

JM: I don't think one can take a single example such as Noah, and therefore conclude that God will always spare His people from catastrophic suffering.

He didn't do it for Christians under Domitian's reign.

He hasn't done it for the Christians in Darfur.

He hasn't done it for the Christians in China.

He didn't do it during the destruction of the Roman Empire.

And Jesus' words in the Olivet Discourse above seem to teach that if His followers are to avoid such suffering, it is up to them to flee from it and wait for the sign of the Coming of the Son of Man.

Only those who have come out of "the tribulation" (the primary characteristic John chose to use to describe life in Christ in Rev. 1:9) via natural death or martyrdom are finally able to rest forever in the presence of God (see the 5th seal in Revelation as well as the description of God's followers and their ultimate destiny in 7:13-17).

The "wiping out" that God's followers will not have to endure will be the one that really counts--the final Judgment!

IV. On the chronology of Revelation

Pre-Trib Disp: *I found this to help explain the Pre-Trib Disp viewpoint on this for those interested:*

The 7 Churches in Revelation: This tradition also views the 7 churches in Revelation as prophecizing the 7 stages in Church history. One interpretation describes these 7 churches as the Patient Church (1st Century), the Persecuted Church (100-316), the Polluted Church (316-500), the Paganized Church (500-1500), the Peculiar Church (1500-1750), the Pure Church (1750-1910) and the Passive Church (1910-?). The present church age is equated with the lukewarm church of Laodicea, as one Brethren writer described:

Whatever interpretation we may take of the book of Revelation, it is undeniable that the church of Laodicea presents a vivid picture of the age in which we now live. Luxury-living abounds on every hand while souls are dying for want of the Gospel of Christ... There is no sense of spiritual need, no longing for true revival...[14]

---

[14] Found at
http://www.deliriumsrealm.com/delirium/articleview.asp?Post=32

This is our condition on the eve of Christ's return.

JM: The biggest problem I see with this interpretation (aside from it having never been held by any interpreter of Revelation up until John Nelson Darby and C.I. Scofield!) is that it is irredeemably subjective and Euro-Amero-centric. What I mean is that these "ages" of the church are not based on anything authoritative or factual. They are simply the view of interpreters in the 19th and 20th centuries of the church in previous centuries.

Furthermore, when you study Church History, you see that these titles only apply to some of the church some of the time. They also only really apply to European and North American experience of Church.

Take for instance the example of they give of the modern church being like the church at Laodicea. Far from being "undeniable", I would argue that it is absolutely deniable that luxury living and spiritual apathy describe the current age of the church-- except maybe in mainline churches in North America and Europe!

The vast majority of Christians live in the southern Hemisphere and are non-European,

non-white. **They are anything BUT representative of Laodicea. Whether it's the underground house churches in China and central Asia, the charismatic churches in Latin America, the indigenous churches in Sub-Saharan Africa, or the fiercely evangelistic churches in Korea, the state of the church in our culture is not justification for imposing these purely futurist labels to the seven churches in Revelation 1-3.**

Pre-Trib Disp: *So then you don't think Revelation is to be read chronologically? Please give some evidence of this non-chronological view.*

JM: Gladly. There are many features in the book which argue strongly for a non-chronological reading. For instance, the cycles of Judgment represented by the 3 sevens (seals, trumpets, bowls) all seem to lead right up until the final judgment, only to then jump back to an earlier point and begin again.

Also, the allegory of the woman, her child, and the dragon depicts broadly the casting down of satan, his attempt to destroy God's people, and God's protection of them from spiritual destruction during their time in a dangerous world where they are aliens and exiles.

Other examples could be given, but they are not recognized by those who first assume that the text must be chronological. Rather, various attempts to chronologize and harmonize all the images are adopted by those seeking to interpret the book through a Dispensational lens.

But if you're interested in Biblical scholarship which demonstrates the often non-chronological nature of Jewish Apocalypse, and specifically Revelation, be sure to check out the following works:

Revelation and the End of All Things by Craig Koester

The Theology of the Book of Revelation by Richard Bauckham

The Throne, the Lamb, and the Dragon by Paul Spilsbury

The Revelation of St. John by G.B. Caird

The Book of Revelation (NIGTC commentary series) by Greg Beale

The Climax of Prophecy by Richard Bauckham

V. On the nature of the Rapture

Pre-Trib Friend: *1 Thessalonians 4:16 says He will "come down from heaven", He won't actually come to earth. This is explained in the next verse where it says, "caught up together with them in the clouds to meet the Lord in the air". To me, this is not the second coming. This is us going to be with Him. It will be a victory procession, because we will at last be at peace in heaven with God.*

JM: This is something I actually agree with you on in principle, just not in timing! This is definitely the language of a victory procession where we meet our conquering Lord and go to be at peace with Him.

However, we don't go back to Heaven with Him; we accompany Him to the New Creation, our glorified/resurrected state of existence with Him on the New Earth.

Pre-Trib Friend: *This sure is a lot to wade through!*

JM: At last something else we totally agree on! :)

Study of eschatology is quite challenging and time-consuming! However, it's something that we are called to do, in order that we may accurately handle the Word of Truth and give a reason to anyone who asks of the faith we have. A lack of proper attention to eschatology was, I believe, the cause of this

reactionary Dispensational Rapture theology that arose in the 1800's.

I believe a healthy, critical, Biblical re-examination is always in order. For instance, I, myself seem to waver between an Historical Premillennial position and an Amillennial one. Both have strengths and both have weaknesses--but both have been embraced by brilliant and Godly Christians in every era of the Church's existence. This cannot be said about the Dispensational Premillennial position—which is one of the primary red flags of which we should take note.

-Eight-
End-Times Eisegesis:
What is it and why does it matter?

For Christians who are seeking to understand what the Bible teaches about the "End Times" there are few things more important than faithfully and accurately interpreting the texts of Scripture in their original contexts before determining any modern meaning or application.

This often involves some hard work and study...but that seems to be how God designed it.

This process of finding the original intended meaning of a text to its original audience is called exegesis (ex-uh-JEE-sis). It means "to draw out", as in to draw out the meaning from the text itself rather than reading our own meaning INTO the text.

That process has a fancy name as well: eisegesis (EYE-suh-jee-sis)...and it is to be avoided as much as possible--particularly by those who find themselves in positions of teaching or spiritual authority.

This point can be illustrated by a prayer letter that was sent out by a very prominent TV ministry to viewers. A church member gave me a copy and asked that I take a look at it.

I was not encouraged by what I read.

[*Note: I am withholding the name of the author and ministry because I don't want this to come across as an attack on any particular individual or ministry, but rather on the method of interpretation used.*]

The letter was a call for Christians to pray for the safety of Israel right now because of Russia and Iran's evil intentions.

Okay...but why not pray for Russia and Iran's people and their safety as well, while we're at it??

However, the petition for prayer wasn't the problem (though it WAS dangerously nationalistic, I felt!). The problem came when the author attempted to provide "Biblical" support for his political, foreign policy position.

Here is an excerpt [with underlines added by me for emphasis]:

> *About 2600 years ago, God gave the Prophet Ezekiel a description of an invasion of Israel after the Jews had been*

re-gathered to the Promised Land from all over the world in the "latter days." Ezekiel wrote of an invasion force led by Russia that would include Iran and "Cush," which is Sudan. The other parties described by Ezekiel that constituted the invading force could include some of the Muslim nations in the former Soviet Caucasus region and possibly Turkey. According to Ezekiel 38:12, they would come seeking "plunder and loot." What greater plunder than the oil riches of the Persian Gulf? Will this unfold all at once? It's difficult to say. But what is clear is this: The Israeli strike against Iran will be the trigger. From then on, dramatic events will follow in quick succession. It all will conclude when God has rained fire on the islands of the sea and on the invading force coming against Israel.

Where will the United States be in all of this conflict? [According to Ezekiel, the "young lions of Tarshish" will be questioning the Russians about their aggression] – questioning, but not acting to stop it. Who are these "young lions of Tarshish?" Tarshish was the region beyond Cadiz in Spain. In antiquity, explorers from Tarshish came to Ireland, then across the ocean to North America, traveling the Mississippi River as far as

112

*the present-day site of Davenport, Iowa. I
believe the term "young lions of Tarshish"
refers to England and the United States of
America. According to Ezekiel, when the
Middle East trouble begins, the young
lions of Tarshish will warn Russia and
Iran, but refuse to act. We will suffer
grave economic damage, but will not
engage in military action to stop the
conflict. However, we may not be spared
nuclear strikes against coastal cities.*

In conclusion, it is my opinion that we
have between 75 and 120 days before
the Middle East starts spinning out of
control. If there was ever a time for
fervent prayer, it is now. Prayer can
change the course of history!

Now while I wholeheartedly agree with that
last sentence, that is about all I could find in
this section of the letter that is truly
Biblically-based!

First of all, it would be helpful to read the
chapter that the author is referring to, Ezekiel
38:

> The word of the LORD came to me: ² "Son
> of man, set your face against Gog, of the
> land of Magog, the chief prince of
> Meshek and Tubal; prophesy against him

³ and say: 'This is what the Sovereign LORD says: I am against you, Gog, chief prince of Meshek and Tubal. ⁴ I will turn you around, put hooks in your jaws and bring you out with your whole army—your horses, your horsemen fully armed, and a great horde with large and small shields, all of them brandishing their swords. ⁵ Persia, Cush and Put will be with them, all with shields and helmets, ⁶ also Gomer with all its troops, and Beth Togarmah from the far north with all its troops—the many nations with you.

⁷ "'Get ready; be prepared, you and all the hordes gathered about you, and take command of them. ⁸ After many days you will be called to arms. In future years you will invade a land that has recovered from war, whose people were gathered from many nations to the mountains of Israel, which had long been desolate. They had been brought out from the nations, and now all of them live in safety. ⁹ You and all your troops and the many nations with you will go up, advancing like a storm; you will be like a cloud covering the land.

¹⁰ "'This is what the Sovereign LORD says: On that day thoughts will come into your mind and you will devise an

evil scheme. [11] You will say, "I will invade a land of unwalled villages; I will attack a peaceful and unsuspecting people—all of them living without walls and without gates and bars. [12] I will plunder and loot and turn my hand against the resettled ruins and the people gathered from the nations, rich in livestock and goods, living at the center of the land." [13] Sheba and Dedan and the merchants of Tarshish and all her villages will say to you, "Have you come to plunder? Have you gathered your hordes to loot, to carry off silver and gold, to take away livestock and goods and to seize much plunder?"'

[14] "Therefore, son of man, prophesy and say to Gog: 'This is what the Sovereign LORD says: In that day, when my people Israel are living in safety, will you not take notice of it? [15] You will come from your place in the far north, you and many nations with you, all of them riding on horses, a great horde, a mighty army. [16] You will advance against my people Israel like a cloud that covers the land. In days to come, Gog, I will bring you against my land, so that the nations may know me when I am proved holy through you before their eyes.

^{17} "'This is what the Sovereign LORD says: You are the one I spoke of in former days by my servants the prophets of Israel. At that time they prophesied for years that I would bring you against them. ^{18} This is what will happen in that day: When Gog attacks the land of Israel, my hot anger will be aroused, declares the Sovereign LORD. ^{19} In my zeal and fiery wrath I declare that at that time there shall be a great earthquake in the land of Israel. ^{20} The fish in the sea, the birds in the sky, the beasts of the field, every creature that moves along the ground, and all the people on the face of the earth will tremble at my presence. The mountains will be overturned, the cliffs will crumble and every wall will fall to the ground. ^{21} I will summon a sword against Gog on all my mountains, declares the Sovereign LORD. Every man's sword will be against his brother. ^{22} I will execute judgment on him with plague and bloodshed; I will pour down torrents of rain, hailstones and burning sulfur on him and on his troops and on the many nations with him. ^{23} And so I will show my greatness and my holiness, and I will make myself known in the sight of many nations. Then they will know that I am the LORD.'

(Ezekiel 38:1-23, NIV)

Now, having read the chapter in question, did you notice that *not once* in the entire chapter do we find any references to Russia, Iran, Sudan, the Soviet Caucasus, or Turkey?

Those modern countries have been READ INTO the text (i.e. eisegeted) in order to fit with the author's idea of what should happen. I've underlined the eisegetical parts above for clarity's sake.

And even if we put aside for the moment that the Hebrew text does not say "the young lions of Tarshish", but rather "Sheba and Dedan and the traders of Tarshish with all their young lions", the much bigger eisegetical error being committed is appealing to the fact that *some* people *may* have moved from Tarshish, Spain to Ireland and then to *parts* of America to indicate that "Tarshish" really means "England and the United States."

This is a bogus journey of interpretation the likes of which would make Bill & Ted proud indeed!

Consider the fact that *millions* of people have settled in the US and England from places like Iran, Russia, Sudan, and Turkey. Using the very same eisegetical line of thinking, one could argue that since the US has people from all those countries, it is actually *America* that is being spoken of as the invading forces in Ezekiel!

But surely the author would not agree with this, would he?

So why then should this reasoning be used to identify the US as "Tarshish"?

My point is that *any* attempt such as this to label modern nations in Biblical texts will *always* result in reading a meaning into the Bible that is simply not there. That is the essence of eisegesis and the complete antithesis of sound Biblical interpretation.

Such imaginary readings go a long way in instilling fear and xenophobia into readers who may not know better and who may simply trust the author because of his fame as a minister (not to mention driving up donations to ministries such as his who seem to be able to "decode" the current political events)...but they do little in the way of teaching the Bible and creating sharp, discerning, learned students of Scripture--which we are *all* called to be.

Even well-known and well-intentioned Christians can fall into error (as can little-known and well-intentioned writers such as myself of course!)...but unfortunately it usually makes it into the media when they do.

This then sends a message to the world that such error makes up what Christians believe or what the Bible teaches. And in a geopolitical climate such as the one we currently inhabit, this is much more serious than "in-house" doctrinal debates among Christians on secondary issues such as Freewill/Predestination or Adult/Infant Baptism.

Those of us who teach and preach from Scripture should be held to the highest standards of scrutiny when it comes to Biblical Interpretation. I know I am not above making interpretive mistakes, and should I ever fall into eisegetical error, I hope others in the Body of Christ are there to guide me back to truth.

"Much will be required of everyone who has been given much. And even more will be expected of the one who has been entrusted with more." --Jesus (Luke 12:48b)

For more on avoiding eisegesis I recommend the following resources:

How to Read the Bible for All Its Worth - Gordon
        Fee & Doug Stuart
Exegetical Fallacies - D.A. Carson
Abusing Scripture – Manfred Brauch
New Testament Exegesis – Gordon Fee
Old Testament Exegesis – Douglas Stuart

-Nine-
Response to an
'End Times' Chain Email

I once received a chain-email during my time as Discipleship Pastor at Good Shepherd. Normally, I just delete these as soon as I see them. But this time I decided to use it as a teaching moment for our congregation.

Here is what I sent out in response (I've kept the original email's content in **bold** below):

Part of being an effective Disciple involves knowing how to discern truth and falsehood and being able to share it with others in a loving way. I received an email earlier this week which I believe provides an excellent opportunity to help equip us all to be the best fishers we can be.

No doubt many of you have received the chain email going around regarding the Bible and Iraq over the past few months. A number of you have asked me about it and it seems that it would be helpful to give a response church-wide so that any of you who receive it in the future will have a Biblical perspective on the matter, and can use the opportunity to discuss true Biblical faith with whomever sends it to you.

Here is the email (in **bold**) along with my comments after each point regarding the numerous errors it contains:

Spooky must read
Pretty interesting read!
Read all of this one, it is interesting!! Read down to the very bottom highlighted in green, you don't want to miss this!

VERY INTERESTING-

1.The Garden of Eden was in Iraq.

>This is misleading to say the least. "Iraq" is a modern political state, not a Biblical location. While the location of Eden is spoken of in Genesis 2, the description is very ambiguous and the names of the rivers are not necessarily the same as they are today. The location of Eden was somewhere in the area between what are now Egypt, Turkey, and Iran.

2. Mesopotamia, which is now Iraq, was the cradle of civilization!

Mesopotamia is not equal to modern day Iraq. It was located partially in what is now modern day Iraq. It is called the cradle of civilization because it is where the oldest surviving remnants of civic artifacts have been discovered (writing, tablets, tools, etc.)

3. Noah built the ark in Iraq.

Again, this is simply not verifiable. The location of where Noah lived and built the ark is nowhere stated in Genesis 6. We are told that the ark came to rest in the hill country of Ararat--however, the Ararat mountains run through modern day Turkey, Syria, Armenia, Iraq and Iran.

4. The Tower of Babel was in Iraq

The exact location of the Tower of Babel is unknown. It was somewhere in the plain of Shinar, which many believe is part of what would later become Babylon.

5. Abraham was from Ur, which is in Southern Iraq!

See comments on #1 above.

6. Isaac's wife Rebekah is from Nahor, which is in Iraq!

Nahor's location is unknown.

124

7. Jacob met Rachel in Iraq.
> Rachel was from Paddam Aram, which is near Haran. Though the exact location is unknown, the area is now part of modern day Syria.

8. Jonah preached in Nineveh - which is in Iraq.
> See comments on #1 above.

9. Assyria, which is in Iraq, conquered the ten tribes of Israel.
> Assyria was an enormous empire that covered much more than "Iraq".

10. Amos cried out in Iraq!
> Amos was from Tekoa in Judah and ministered in and around Bethel. He was never in "Iraq."

11. Babylon, which is in Iraq, destroyed Jerusalem.
> See comments on #1 above.

12. Daniel was! In [sic] the lion's den in Iraq!
> See comments on #1 above.

13. The three Hebrew children were in the fire in Iraq (Jesus had been in Iraq also as the fourth person in the Fiery furnace!)

See comments on #1 above. Also, the identity of the 4th individual in the fiery furnace, while thought by some to be the pre-incarnate Christ, is identified only as "one like a son of the gods", an ancient near east way of saying "Angel."

14. Belshazzar, the King of Babylon saw the "writing on the wall" in Iraq.

See comments on #1 above.

15.   Nebuchadnezzar, King of Babylon, carried the Jews captive into Iraq.

See comments on #1 above.

16. Ezekiel preached in Iraq.

See comments on #1 above.

17. The wise men were from Iraq

This is not true. Nowhere is the origin of the magi specified. They came "from the east." That is as specific as Scripture gets regarding their origin. By the time of Jesus, "magi" was a term generally applied to fortune tellers and esoteric religious cults throughout the Mediterranean world. (See: *The Archaeological Study Bible*, footnote 2.1, p.1560)

18. Peter preached in Iraq.

This is not found anywhere in the New Testament.

19. The "Empire of Man" described in Revelation is called Babylon, which was a city in Iraq!
See comments on #1 above.

And you have probably seen this one. Israel is the nation most often mentioned in the Bible. But do you know which nation is second? It is Iraq! However, that is not the name that is used in the Bible The names used in the Bible are Babylon, Land of Shinar, and Mesopotamia . The word Mesopotamia means between the two rivers, more exactly between the Tigris and Euphrates Rivers. The name Iraq, means country with deep roots.

Indeed Iraq is a country with deep roots and is a very significant country in the Bible.
See comments on #1 above. The modern political state known as "Iraq" has absolutely zero significance in the Bible.

No other nation, except Israel, has more history and prophecy associated it than Iraq.
See comments on #1 above. There is not a single prophecy in the Bible associated with "Iraq."

And also, this is something to think about!
Since America is typically represented by an eagle. Saddam should have read up on his Muslim passages...

The following verse is from the Koran, (the Islamic Bible)

Koran (9:11) - For it is written that a son of Arabia would awaken a fearsome Eagle. The wrath of the Eagle would be felt throughout the lands of Allah and lo, while some of the people trembled in despair still more rejoiced; for the wrath of the Eagle cleansed the lands of Allah;
And there was peace.

(Note the verse number!) Hmmmmmmm?!
This is completely and utterly false. Surah 9:11 in the Qur'an is about agreements made with idolaters. The actual verse reads:

"But if they [the idolaters] repent and keep up prayer and pay the poor-rate, they are your brethren in faith; and we make the communications clear for a people who know."   --SURAH 9:11

The fact that this email "bears false witness" against the text of the Qur'an, along with all of the erroneous claims made throughout, is enough to demonstrate that whoever composed it is acting deceitfully and is bringing shame upon the name of Jesus.

More than that, however, is the blatant appeal to superstition (which is directly spoken against in Scripture) that follows below:

I BETTER NOT HEAR OF ANYONE BREAKING THIS ONE OR SEE DELETED. This is a ribbon for soldiers fighting in Iraq. Pass it on to everyone and pray. Something good will happen to you tonight at 11:11 PM. This is not a joke! Someone will either call you or will talk to you online and say that they love you. Do not break this chain. Send this to 13 people in the next 15 minutes. Go.

Chain emails such as the one above do nothing but tarnish the reputation of any Christian who sends them. We, as children of the light, must walk in that light and reject deceit and slander of any kind--even if it's directed against another Faith, such as Islam.

This type of "spiritualizing" of a current political situation is both ignorant and dangerous. We must remember that we will be held accountable for every careless word uttered (or typed!). Christians should strive to be a body of believers who are passionately committed to the Truth of God's Word. In the future, if you receive a chain email like this, instead of forwarding it on, take the opportunity to reflect on the call to honesty and the responsibility that comes with handling the Word of God.

Your fellow Disciple,
JM

-Ten-
The Danger of 'Standing With Israel'... Or Any Other Modern Government

Recently I saw a picture on a friend's Facebook page that had a drawing of the Star of David with the words "I STAND WITH ISRAEL" imposed over it.

Artistically, it was pretty.

Theologically, it was very troubling.

Why?

Because I believe Christians (and even Jews) who proudly boast of "standing with Israel" *as a modern nation* are in danger of borderline idolatry–by both Old and New Testament standards.

Now, that's an incredibly controversial thing to say...so allow me to clarify what I mean.

But first, a disclaimer:

ANYTIME one attempts to speak to the situation regarding the states of Israel and Palestine (I choose to acknowledge both Israeli AND Palestinian claims to statehood), there will ALWAYS be backlash–particularly if one brings issues of theology into the discussion. However, it is a VERY important discussion to have and we must not be afraid to engage the issue head-on...particularly those of us who claim to follow the Jewish Messiah! That being said, disagreement and criticism are always to be expected. But personal attacks or flippant use of inflammatory and unhelpful labels (such as "anti-Semitic" or "godless") toward those with whose view we disagree are unacceptable to any true follower of Jesus.

Okay, back to the discussion...

The nation that exists today in the Middle East with the blue and white Star of David as its flag is a secular state. Its Constitution is not based on Torah, but rather on Western democratic ideals and a European/American form of government. I don't know many people who would dispute this—in fact, most who support Israel are quite proud of this very thing!

However, because it was named "Israel" when it was established in the mid-20th century, many Christians saw it as the reconstitution of Biblical Israel...and thus as a divinely-sanctioned nation that was to be a key event in ushering in the return of Christ.

In fact, most evangelical Christians claimed it as a "miracle" (despite the fact that after WWII, politically and militarily speaking, there was very little that could be said to be "miraculous" about superpowers with modern weaponry establishing a country in land they controlled) and "fulfilled prophecy" (despite there being very little in the actual details of the events which could be correlated with Biblical prophecy in anything more than a superficial or vague manner).

Understandably, then, those who saw the formation (or "ingathering" as they might rather call it) of Israel in this manner would have a favorable view towards this new nation. And since in just the previous decade the Jewish people had suffered tremendous horror in the form of Shoah (the Holocaust), the world was rightly sympathetic to the plight of the Jewish people and many believed they deserved a homeland where they would be able to live free from fear of attack or persecution.

Through political maneuvering and negotiation between the victorious powers of WWII and the European community, it was decided that the place for this new nation of Israel would be the land in the Middle East where Biblical Israel once lived. It seemed only logical.

The only problem was that during the nearly 2,000 years in which the Jewish people had been spread over the face of the earth as a result of Jerusalem's destruction by the Romans, many other people had continued to live in that very land, including a number of Jews of Middle Eastern descent (In fact, a friend of mine whose family was forced to flee Israel in the 1940s can trace her family's ancestry back to 1st century Christians in Jerusalem!).

Needless to say, when this massive influx of Europeans arrived in the new nation of "Israel", there was a good bit of conflict with those–both Jews and Arabs–who were already there.

[**Note: This is a VERY simplified summary and I am intentionally avoiding getting into the numerous historical nuances of the past 60+ years, both because it is beyond the scope of this chapter and because there are many accounts with varying degrees of bias to which interested readers should refer.**]

However, despite being established as a homeland for the Jewish people, at no point in time has the nation of Israel ever been established according to the Covenant given by God at Mt. Sinai.

Rather, many of the earliest and most influential leaders of this new state (often referred to as "Zionists", to distinguish the political goals they sought from the religious aspects of "Judaism"), such as Theodor Herzl, were mostly secular European Jews who were quite clear that they had little use for Torah's commandments, other than for their religious symbolic value in gaining support among the larger Jewish and Christian world population.[15] Incidentally, there were and always have been a vocal minority of devout Jews who openly oppose Zionism in principle because they believe that the true return of the Jews from exile cannot happen apart from the coming of Messiah.[16]

So, despite claims to the contrary by many prominent and prolific voices among Conservative Christian Zionists[17], the nation of *Israel as a nation* cannot be said to have legitimate claim to the promises given to *Biblical Covenant Israel*. This is a CRUCIAL

---

[15] (see http://atheism.about.com/library/glossary/judaism/bldef_zionism.htm for more on the secular roots of Zionism).

[16] For more on this, see "*A Threat from Within: A Century of Jewish Opposition to Zionism*" by Yakov Rabkin.

[17] For example: http://jmsmith.org/blog/this-is-why-bad-theology-matters/

distinction...and one that many of my fellow evangelical Christians often seem to miss.[18]

"But wait...what about the famous promise to Abraham's offspring? Didn't God say flat-out that He would bless those who bless the nation of Israel and curse those who curse them??"

Well...actually...No.

He did not.

Let's look at the often-cited passage from Genesis:

> *"Now the LORD said to Abram,*
> *"Go forth from your country,*
> *And from your relatives*
> *And from your father's house,*
> *To the land which I will show you;*
> *and I will make you a great nation,*
> *and I will bless you,*
> *and make your name great;*
> *and so you shall be a blessing;*
> *and I will bless those who bless you,*
> *and the one who curses you I will curse.*

---

[18] For an incredibly thought-provoking and level-headed discussion of this issue by Jewish Psychologist Mark Braverman, see the following post in Disciple Dojo: A Jewish voice that needs to be heard by Christians.

> *and in you all the families of the earth shall be blessed."*

(Gen 12:1-3 NAS)

This is God speaking to Abram (who would later be renamed "Abraham") about His plan to reconcile ALL THE NATIONS OF THE EARTH back to Himself. This is one of the most foundational promises in all of Scripture. It is the "Big Idea" of the Bible.[19]

This initial promise is later confirmed by God to Abraham and extended to all of Abraham's "seed":

> *"Now when Abram was ninety-nine years old, the LORD appeared to Abram and said to him, "I am God Almighty; Walk before Me, and be blameless and I will establish My covenant between Me and you, and I will multiply you exceedingly."*
>
> *And Abram fell on his face, and God talked with him, saying, "As for Me, behold, My covenant is with you, and you shall be the father of a multitude of nations.*

---

[19] For an in-depth look at this passage reflecting the overall grand narrative of the Bible, I can't recommend Christopher Wright's magisterial book "*The Mission of God*" strongly enough!

*No longer shall your name be called
Abram, but your name shall be Abraham;
For I will make you the father of a
multitude of nations.
And I will make you exceedingly fruitful,
and I will make nations of you,
and kings shall come forth from you.*

*And I will establish My covenant
between Me and you and your
descendants [Heb. "seed"] after you
throughout their generations for an
everlasting covenant, to be God to you
and to your descendants [Heb. "seed"]
after you.*

*And I will give to you and to your
descendants after you, the land of your
sojournings, all the land of Canaan, for
an everlasting possession; and I will be
their God.""* (Gen 17:1-8 NAS)

There are many things—entire semesters'
worth, in fact!—that could be said about the
passages above. However, what matters most,
at least for Christians, is what the New
Testament writers said about them.

Look at what Paul, himself a Pharisee who knew the Hebrew Scripture by heart, said about God's promise to Abraham and his "seed":

> *"Now the promises were spoken to Abraham **and to his seed**. He does not say, "And to seeds," as referring to many, **but rather to one, "And to your seed," that is, Christ.**"* (Gal 3:16 NAS)

> *"And if you belong to Christ, **then you are Abraham's offspring, heirs according to promise.**"*
> (Gal 3:29 NAS)

This is one of the deepest and most profound teachings of the entire Bible. It has generated thousands of pages of commentary by some of the finest minds in history. However, I only want to point out a few key observations:

- **The promise of blessings and curses are given to Abraham and his "seed"**
- **Abraham's "seed" would include a "multitude of nations"**
- **Jesus, as Israel's Messiah, is the culmination and embodiment of all the promises given to Israel by God, and thus the true "seed" of Abraham**
- **Those who are united with Israel's Messiah in covenant faith are heirs to**

the promise–regardless of their ethnicity or earthly citizenship

Of course, in light of the New Testament, we are to love and support *the Jewish people*, which includes seeing to it that no one ever threatens them with genocide or other horrors like they have endured over the centuries ever again (much of it, as my friend Dr. Michael Brown has documented in his book "*Our Hands Are Stained With Blood*", has shamefully come by the hands of people professing to follow Jesus!).

But we do so because they are created in God's image and are dearly loved by Him; not because we'll "be cursed" if we don't. God is definitely not done with the Jewish people–as some throughout Church history have erroneously taught! He still has a unique plan for the "descendents of Abraham according to the flesh."

But it does not follow from any of this that Christians are called to "stand with" the modern nation of Israel.

To equate modern Israel with the Jewish people is theologically wrong and, I would argue, very irresponsible...especially given the fact that modern Israel is a *thoroughly secular* (i.e. non-religious!) nation which engages in a number of practices and policies which are not in line with Torah itself.

For instance, according to Torah:

> *"When a stranger resides with you in your land, you shall not do him wrong. The stranger who resides with you shall be to you as the native among you, and you shall love him as yourself; for you were aliens in the land of Egypt: I am the LORD your God."* (Lev 19:33-34 NAS)

Thus, regardless of how bad the nations surrounding Israel may be, this cannot be used as justification for mistreatment or prejudiced policies regarding Palestinians.

Yet, as even many Israelis point out[20], Palestinians are systematically treated as suspicious, at best, and enemies at worst by the Israeli government. Anyone who claims otherwise would do well to spend a year living in the Palestinian territories...they will likely change their minds as a result!

Furthermore, according to Torah, Israel was only allowed to occupy the land so long as they kept the Sinai Covenant. Breaking the Covenant was grounds for eviction from the

---

[20] See, for example, http://www.btselem.org/

142

land itself, just as the previous inhabitants had been evicted due to their sin:

> *"You are therefore to keep all My statutes and all My ordinances and do them, so that the land to which I am bringing you to live will not spew you out."* (Lev 20:22 NAS)

Now, no matter how much we may agree with or approve of modern Israel's form of government from a political perspective, it is no more based on Torah than the U.S. Constitution is based on the Sermon on the Mount.

Nor is the modern state of Israel submitted to that which Torah points–the New Covenant of the Messiah Jesus. Despite the efforts of various Jewish brothers and sisters in Christ in sharing the Gospel of Yeshua with their fellow Jews in ways that do not advocate abandoning one's "Jewishness" (the best of which can be found, once again in the "*Answering Jewish Objections to Jesus*" volumes by my previously mentioned friend Dr. Michael Brown[21]), the

---

[21] I have a TREMENDOUS amount of respect for Dr. Brown and consider him not only a good friend, but also an incredible scholar with a first-rate mind who I am deeply indebted to in my own theological development. He and do not see eye-to-eye on a number of issues regarding the current state of Israel, but that does not in any way diminish the admiration I have for him and his ministry. In fact, it is through my conversations with him and other Messianic friends that I have been spurred continually to sharper thinking and more

numbers of Christians and Messianic Jews in Israel remains very small.

Hopefully, however, this continues to change—in fact, some friends who minister frequently in Israel tell me that there are very encouraging signs of revival taking place on both sides of the wall. But as of right now, by both Old and New Testament standards, *the modern secular state* known as "Israel" can in no way be said to have God's unconditional Covenant blessing.

Furthermore, even when Israel *was* under Torah (that is, during the Hebrew Monarchy and 2nd Temple period), there was never a one-to-one correspondence between supporting them militarily and receiving blessing from God. In fact, Prophets such as Jeremiah were often persecuted *precisely because* they spoke out against the nation of Israel...and their persecutors were those who, regardless of the nation's behavior, were most definitely "standing with Israel"!

This is why, *even from a Hebrew Bible perspective*, one cannot justify an unconditional support of Israel as a nation–

---

careful historical, theological and political study of the Israeli-Palestinian conflict. But our areas of agreement and unity in our Messiah FAR surpass any disagreements we may have! This is very much an "in-house" conversation.

particularly when such "support" comes primarily in the form of billions of dollars worth of bombers and bulldozers.

"Okay...so are you saying we should 'stand with Palestine' then?!"

No.

I'm certainly not.

Like modern Israel, modern Palestine is also an earthly political state. While I may *personally* believe Palestinians have been on the receiving end of a greater degree of violence (be it from early Zionist militias, modern militant settlers, or IDF bombs and bullets), I do not believe this in any way exonerates the state of Palestine from wrongdoing, nor does it automatically render them the "good guys" (as many anti-Israel proponents often argue).

Palestinian leaders and radicals bear a large measure of guilt in this ongoing conflict and this should not be downplayed by those who are sympathetic to their cause. Hatred and terrorism should never be justified by appealing to hatred and terrorism on the part of one's enemy!

But these facts remain:

- **ALL modern political states are a mixed bag.**
- **ALL modern political states are earthly powers.**
- **Jesus specifically said that His Kingdom (that is, the Kingdom of God!) was not of this world.**
- **Jesus did not "stand with" Israel's leadership anymore so than he did with Rome's.**
- **Jesus knew that being Abraham's "seed" was a matter of devotion to God and covenant faith, not ethnicity or earthly citizenship.**

Why then do modern Christians have such a hard time living this out when it comes to Israel and Palestine (or Iran, or China, or Russia, or America, or North Korea, or *insert 'bad guy' country of choice*)?? Why do we ignore the *clear* teachings of the Bible ("*love your neighbor as yourself*" in Torah, interpreted as "*love your enemy*" by Jesus) in favor of folk-theology or esoteric "End Times" scenarios that require an engineering degree to chart out properly, but which show little, if any, regard in particular for Palestinian followers of Jesus??[22]

---

[22] Thankfully prominent evangelical voices, such as John Piper, are starting to speak out publicly against this tendency among Western Christians. http://jmsmith.org/blog/thank-you-john-piper/

I would suggest it's because many of us want quick, sound-byte answers.

We want to know who the "good guys" are and who to "stand with"...rather than having to do the complicated, tiresome, and challenging work of being a true peacemaker!

I would also suggest it's because we have a natural tendency to identify with those who are more "like us", either in terms of ethnicity, socio-economic status, form of government, or cultural outlook.

"We" are the good guys..."they" *must* therefore be the "bad guys" because "they" are not "us!"

Yet these are the very walls that the Gospel continually seeks to tear down!

Bottom line: **When we choose to "stand with" a modern nation–*even one named "Israel"*–we often end up unintentionally "standing against" the God of Abraham, Isaac, and Jacob...as well as our Jewish Messiah.**

The potential irony should *at the very least* give us pause in our political/military/sociological convictions, should it not?

As Christians, we are free to gravitate toward policies or endorse political outlooks which we believe honor God and demonstrate love for neighbor (keeping in mind Jesus' definition of "neighbor" is often quite different than ours!), but we must never seek to baptize those ideologies or political views which openly favor one modern geopolitical nation over another by appealing to Scriptural proof-texts.

To do so is to mishandle the Sword of the Spirit and risk wounding ourselves and others in the process.

The situation with Israel and Palestine is a highly complicated one; anyone who believes otherwise is either misinformed or woefully naive. But it is for this very reason that we must resist the urge to sanctify "our side"–be it that of Israel, Palestine or any other modern nation. It's hard to maintain such balance...but that is what we are called to do as peacemakers!

In fact, it is the "peacemakers", rather than those who "stand with Israel", who Israel's Messiah Himself said were to be "blessed" (Matt.5:9).

If we must "stand with" anyone, may we it be with the Prince of Peace rather than the flag of a nation...regardless of the colors.

-Appendix A-
An Open Letter To American Christians

The following letter written by Andrew Miller and myself was originally published by 972mag.com, an independent online newspaper that covers issues involving human rights in Israel and Palestine. The original post along with the heated comments it generated can be found at http://972mag.com/dear-fellow-american-christians-speak-up-against-suffering/36719/

Dear fellow American Christians: Speak up against suffering

By Andrew Miller and James-Michael Smith

Blessed are the peacemakers, for they shall be called sons of God. —Matthew 5:9

We are writing to you, our fellow Christians from the United States, with which the State of Israel has enjoyed a unique relationship since its founding, because we are concerned with the nature of support that many American Christians provide for Israel's policies.

Like you, we support the right of Israel to exist and thrive, to be a democracy based on principles of justice described in the Law and the Prophets, and to live in peace with its neighbors.

Like you, we feel a deep reverence for the land in which many of the Hebrew prophets, and Jesus himself, lived and spoke.

And like you, we deeply respect the Jewish people for preserving the Hebrew Bible, for the immense suffering that they have valiantly endured, and for so many other reasons.

Unfortunately, this is not enough for many of our fellow Christians. For them, being truly "pro-Israel" seems to mean that one must never suggest that Israelis could do more than they currently do to live in peace with their closest neighbors.

We are concerned that leaders such as Mac Hammond, Gary Bauer, and John Hagee regularly criticize any suggestion that Israel's policies could take better account of the rights of Palestinians living within the territories that Israel occupied in 1967. It disheartens us that such leaders often justify discrimination against Palestinians by painting all of them as terrorists. While violence against innocent civilians is a major concern, statistics show that the vast majority of Palestinians have nothing to do with it.

It troubles us that we cannot tell from the public rhetoric of such leaders if they really believe that Palestinians, like Israeli Jews, are human beings made in the image of God, and therefore worthy of the same fundamental rights. It concerns us that such voices regularly accuse anyone who advocates for the creation of a sovereign state of Palestine that will live in peace with Israel as being "anti-Israel", "hostile" to Israel, or worse.

Please consider organizations such as B'Tselem[23], Machsom Watch[24], Yesh Din[25], and Gisha[26].

Each is run (primarily or fully) by Israeli Jews. It is unreasonable to accuse these organizations of being "hostile" to their own country. Each has taken painstaking care, over many years, to document and protest widespread violations of the rights of innocent Palestinians by the Israeli military and/or settlers in the West Bank and Gaza. These violations include severe restrictions on

---

[23] http://www.btselem.org/English/index.asp
[24] http://www.machsomwatch.org/en/
[25] http://www.yesh-din.org/
[26] http://www.gisha.org/

movement; systematic theft of land, water, and other resources; arbitrary detention of children; torture, and many others.

To the extent that self-critical human rights organizations like these flourish within Israel, they are one indication that Israel is a robust democracy. Along with millions of other Christians around the world, we very much want this democracy to continue to exist and to thrive.

But the fact that Israel consistently oppresses innocent Palestinians in the occupied territories can't be ignored. There is simply too much documentation.

Part of the reason that there is so little discussion of the rights of Palestinians among American Christians seems to be that many believe that the Bible tells us to provide unwavering support for Israel's policies, regardless of how it actually treats non-Jews. One serious problem with this view is that it ignores the fact that the government of Israel, like any other government, is composed of human beings who might be capable of making mistakes.

Another problem is that this view misrepresents the focus of the Bible. It is based on prophetic passages that are difficult, if not impossible to interpret with precision, but it ignores straightforward passages such as the following:

> For the LORD your God... shows no partiality nor takes a bribe. He administers justice for the fatherless and the widow, and loves the stranger, giving him food and clothing. Therefore love the stranger, for you were strangers in the land of Egypt.
>
> —Deuteronomy 10:17-19

Perhaps the biggest problem with such views, however, is that they force many American Christians to avoid showing solidarity with the Palestinian Christians living in the occupied territories.

If one listened only to American Christians, one might never realize that there has historically been a large Christian presence among Arabic-speaking Palestinians. Here are some of the basics of this history: http://en.wikipedia.org/wiki/Palestinian_Chris tians,%20http:/news.bbc.co.uk/2/hi/middle_ east/4499668.stm

Looking at the data, a number of facts become clear.

First, tens of thousands of Palestinian Christians still live in the West Bank. Many live in the area around Bethlehem, the birthplace of Christ.

Second, like most Palestinians in the West Bank, Christians there suffer various forms of oppression from the Israeli military occupation.

Third, the number of West Bank Christians has fallen dramatically since 1967.[27] They cite the occupation of the West Bank as largely responsible for the mass exodus of Christians from their ancestral homes.

Fourth, some of these Palestinian Christians are evangelicals, and they accept precisely the same doctrinal statements as American evangelical Christians.

Fifth, American evangelicals have, as a community, done little to advocate for the rights of Christians living in Bethlehem and the rest of the West Bank. Rather, the most visible efforts of evangelical leaders have

---

[27] http://www.haaretz.com/news/national/declining-palestinian-christian-population-fears-its-churches-are-turning-into-museums-1.317689

been directed at labeling people who speak up for the rights of Christians (and other Palestinians) as "anti-Israel," "hostile" to Israel, etc.

In this and other ways, *American Christians have contributed to discrimination against tens of thousands of Christians in the Holy Land, and have contributed to the exodus of tens of thousands more Christians from their ancestral homes.*

This situation is intolerable. Very soon, one of us will be traveling to Bethlehem to participate in a conference hosted by Palestinian evangelical Christians who live there.[28] It breaks our hearts to participate knowing that our community has contributed to the suffering of our Palestinian Christian brothers and sisters who live so close to Christ's birthplace.

If we could express our hearts to you, our fellow American Christians, we would say the following: First, please stop spending so much time trying to apply with precision the imagery and symbolism of the Bible, particularly the Apocalyptic passages. It is good to support Israel's right to flourish, but it is also good to do so without trying to help

---

[28] http://www.christatthecheckpoint.com/

God bring about the battle of Armageddon. God does not need our help to fulfill his predictions.

Second, please pay attention to those things that God wants us to pay attention to. The prophets of old make it clear that God wants us to focus on seeking impartial justice, supporting the disadvantaged, seeking true *shalom*, and other such actions, which they emphasized over and over again.

Finally, when you see American Christians justifying discrimination against innocent Palestinians (Christians or otherwise), *speak up*. Explain to them why this is unhealthy for us, as well as for both Palestinians and Israelis. We are showing friendship to no one when we allow the oppression of the innocent to go unchallenged.

In closing, please consider again the following passages from the Biblical Prophets. They are only a small sample among many, many others that speak the same message...

> *And if a stranger dwells with you in your land, you shall not mistreat him. The stranger who dwells among you shall be to you as one born among you, and you*

shall love him as yourself; for you were strangers in the land of Egypt: I am the LORD your God.

-Leviticus 19:33-34

For if... you do not oppress the stranger, the fatherless, and the widow, and do not shed innocent blood in this place, or walk after other gods to your hurt, then I will cause you to dwell in this place, in the land that I gave to your fathers forever and ever.

-Jeremiah 7:5-7

Therefore, because you tread down the
       poor
And take grain taxes from him....
Afflicting the just and taking bribes,
Diverting the poor from justice at the
       gate...
Woe to you who desire the day of the
       LORD!
For what good is the day of the LORD to
       you?...
But let justice run down like water,
And righteousness like a mighty stream.

-Amos 5:11-24

James-Michael ("JM") Smith is a graduate of Gordon-Conwell Theological Seminary and author of "Cleansed and Abiding: A Proposed View of Christian Perfection." He is the founder of Disciple Dojo (JMSmith.org), an ecumenical discipleship resource ministry.

Andrew Miller is an American Christian living in Bordeaux, France. He blogs (sometimes) at http://andrewsbethlehemblog.wordpress.com/ and elsewhere.

-Appendix B-
JM's Translation of Revelation
for Personal Study & Teaching

The following is a translation of the book of Revelation which I prepared and which is used in Disciple Dojo's "Revelation: A Guided Tour of the Apocalypse" DVD curriculum.[29]

I have noted in parentheses certain key Greek terms which have interpretive significance.

I have also laid out the text in a way that helps readers see the relationship of various clauses and the overall "flow" of the book.

Lastly, whenever John quotes or strongly alludes to passages from the Hebrew Bible (Old Testament), I have included the reference in bold in parentheses beside it. This is to enable the reader to easily find the passage when studying and also gives a visual impression of just how heavily Revelation is influenced by the imagery and message of the Hebrew Scriptures.

There are many excellent translations out there and by no means am I claiming this to be superior to any of them. It's simply one I put together so that I could distribute it to

---

[29] Available at http://jmsmith.org/store/revelation

students of my Revelation course for their use in note-taking and without having to worry about any copyright issues that would arise if I had used any modern translations in print.

1:1 The revelation (Ἀποκάλυψις) of Jesus the Messiah,

      which God gave him

      to show his servants what must take place soon/swiftly (ἐν τάχει).

He signified it (ἐσήμανεν) by sending his angel to his servant John,

[2] who then testified (ἐμαρτύρησεν) to everything that he saw concerning the word of God and the testimony (μαρτυρίαν) of Jesus the Messiah.

[3] Blessed is the one who reads the words of this prophecy aloud, and blessed are those who hear and obey the things written in it, because the time is near!

[4] From John, to the 7 churches that are in the province of Asia:

      Grace and peace to you from
          the one who is,
            and who was,
              and who is coming,
      and from the 7 spirits
          who are before his throne,
      [5] and from Jesus Christ–
          the faithful witness (μάρτυς),
          the firstborn from among the dead,
          the ruler over the kings of the earth.

To the one who loves us and has set us free from our sins at the cost of his own blood [6] and has appointed us as a kingdom, as priests serving his God and Father--[to him] be the glory and the power for ever and ever!

      Amen!

[7] Look! **He is coming with the clouds**, (Dan. 7:13)

and **every eye will see him,**
> **even those who pierced him** (Zech. 12:10),

and all the tribes on the earth will mourn because of him. Yes indeed!
Amen!

[8] "I am the Alpha and the Omega," says the Lord God–
> the one who is,
>> and who was,
>>> and who is coming–
> the All-Powerful! (παντοκράτωρ)

[9] I, John, (your brother and companion in the tribulation (θλίψει), kingdom, and patient endurance that are in Jesus) was on the island called Patmos because of the word of God and the testimony (μαρτυρίαν) of Jesus.

[10] I was in the Spirit on the Lord's Day when I heard behind me a loud voice like a trumpet, [11] saying:
> *"Write in a book/scroll what you see and send it to the 7 churches– to Ephesus, Smyrna, Pergamum, Thyatira, Sardis, Philadelphia, and Laodicea."*

[12] I turned to see whose voice was speaking to me, and when I did so, I saw 7 golden menorahs, [13] and in the midst of the menorahs was **one like a son of man** (Dan. 7:13).

He was dressed in a robe extending down to his feet
> and he wore a wide golden belt around his chest.
[14] His head and hair were as white as wool, even as white as snow,
> and his eyes were like a fiery flame.
[15] His feet were like polished bronze refined in a furnace, and his voice was like the roar of many waters.

[16] He held 7 stars in his right hand,
and a sharp double-edged sword extended out
of his mouth.
His face shone like the sun shining at full strength.

[17] When I saw him I fell down at his feet as though I were dead, but he placed his right hand on me and said:

"*Do not be afraid! I am the first and the last,*
[18] *and the one who lives!*
I was dead, but look, now I am alive! Forever and ever!
And I hold the keys of death and of Hades!
[19] *Therefore write*
what you saw (ἃ εἶδες),
what they are (ἃ εἰσὶν),
and what is about to happen
(ἃ μέλλει γενέσθαι) *after these things* (μετὰ ταῦτα).

[20] *The mystery of the 7 stars that you saw in my right hand and the 7 golden menorahs is this: The 7 stars are the angels of the 7 churches and the 7 menorahs are the 7 churches.*

2:1 "*To the angel of the church in* Ephesus, *write the following*:

"This is the solemn pronouncement of the one who has a firm grasp on the 7 stars in his right hand— the one who walks among the 7 golden menorahs:
[2] 'I know your works as well as your labor and steadfast endurance, and that you cannot tolerate evil. You have even put to the test those calling themselves Apostles (but are not!), and have discovered that they are false.

164

³ I am also aware that you have persisted steadfastly, endured much for the sake of my name, and have not grown weary.

⁴ But I have this against you: You have departed from your first love! ⁵ Therefore, remember from what high state you have fallen and repent! Do the deeds you did at the first; if not, I will come to you and remove your menorah from its place– that is, if you do not repent.

⁶ But you do have this going for you: You hate what the Nicolaitans practice– practices that I also hate.

⁷ Let the ones having ears hear what the Spirit says to the churches. To the one who conquers, I will permit him to eat from the tree of life that is in the paradise of God.'

⁸ "To the angel of the church in _Smyrna_ write the following:

"This is the solemn pronouncement of the one who is the first and the last, the one who was dead, but came to life:

⁹ 'I know the distress you are suffering and your poverty--but you are rich! I also know the slander against you by those who are calling themselves Jews but are not (but are a synagogue of Satan!) ¹⁰ Do not be afraid of the things you are about to suffer. The devil is about to have some of you thrown into prison so you may be tested, and you will experience suffering for 10 days. <u>Remain faithful even to the point of death, and I will give you the crown that is life itself</u>.

¹¹ Let the ones having ears hear what the Spirit says to the churches. The one who conquers (ὁ νικῶν) will in no way be harmed by the second death.'

¹² "To the angel of the church in _Pergamum_ write the following:

"This is the solemn pronouncement of the one who has the sharp double-edged sword:
¹³ 'I know where you live– where Satan's throne is. Yet you continue to cling to my name and you have not denied your faith in me, even in the days of Antipas, my faithful witness, who was killed in your city where Satan lives.
¹⁴ But I have a few things against you: You have some people there who follow the teaching of Balaam, who instructed Balak to put a stumbling block before the people of Israel so they would eat food sacrificed to idols and commit sexual immorality. ¹⁵ In the same way, there are also some among you who follow the teaching of the Nicolaitans.
¹⁶ Therefore, repent! If not, I will come against you quickly and make war against those people with the sword of my mouth.
¹⁷ Let the ones having ears hear what the Spirit says to the churches. To the one who conquers, I will give him some of the hidden manna, and I will give him a white stone, and on that stone will be written a new name that no one can understand except the one who receives it.'

¹⁸ *"To the angel of the church in Thyatira write the following:*

"This is the solemn pronouncement of the Son of God, the one who has eyes like a fiery flame and whose feet are like polished bronze:
¹⁹ 'I know your deeds: your love, faith, service, and steadfast endurance. In fact, your more recent deeds are greater than your earlier ones.
²⁰ But I have this against you: You tolerate that woman Jezebel, who calls herself a prophetess, and by her teaching deceives my servants to commit sexual immorality and to eat food sacrificed to idols. ²¹ I have given her time to repent, but she is not willing to repent of her sexual immorality.

²² Look! I am throwing her onto a bed of violent illness, and those who commit adultery with her into terrible suffering, unless they repent of her deeds. ²³ Furthermore, I will strike her followers with a deadly disease, and then all the churches will know that I am the one who searches minds and hearts. I will repay each one of you what your deeds deserve.

²⁴ But to the rest of you in Thyatira, all who do not hold to this teaching (who have not learned the so-called "deep secrets of Satan"), to you I say: I do not put any additional burden on you. ²⁵ However, hold on to what you have until I come.

²⁶ And to the one who conquers and who continues in my deeds until the end, I will give him authority over the nations–

²⁷ he will rule *them with an iron rod*

and like clay jars he will break them to pieces (cf. Psalm 2:8-9), ²⁸ just as I have received the right to rule from my Father– and I will give him the morning star.

²⁹ Let the ones having ears hear what the Spirit says to the churches.'

3:1 "*To the angel of the church in* Sardis *write the following:*

"This is the solemn pronouncement of the one who holds the 7 spirits of God and the 7 stars:

'I know your deeds, that you have a reputation that you are alive, but in reality you are dead. ² Wake up then, and strengthen what remains that was about to die, because I have not found your deeds complete in the sight of my God.

³ Therefore, remember what you received and heard, and obey it, and repent. If you do not wake up, I will come like a thief, and you will never know at what hour I will come against you.

⁴ But you have a few individuals in Sardis who have not stained their clothes, and they will walk with me dressed in white, because they are worthy. ⁵ The

one who conquers will be dressed like them in white clothing, and I will never erase his name from the book of life, but will declare his name before my Father and before his angels.

⁶ Let the ones having ears hear what the Spirit says to the churches.'

⁷ "*To the angel of the church in Philadelphia write the following:*

"This is the solemn pronouncement of the Holy One, the True One, who holds the key of David, who opens doors no one can shut, and shuts doors no one can open:

⁸ 'I know your deeds. Look! I have put in front of you an open door that no one can shut. I know that you have little strength, but you have obeyed my word and have not denied my name.

⁹ Listen! I am going to make those people from the synagogue of Satan who say they are Jews but *are not—but are lying*! Look!—I will make them come and bow down at your feet and acknowledge that I have loved you. ¹⁰ Because you have kept my admonition to endure steadfastly, I will also keep you from the hour of testing that is about to come upon all mankind to test the ones living on the earth (κατοικοῦντας ἐπὶ τῆς γῆς).

¹¹ I am coming soon/swiftly. Hold on to what you have so that no one can take away your crown. ¹² The one who conquers I will make a pillar in the temple of my God, and he will never depart from it. I will write on him the name of my God and the name of the city of my God (the New Jerusalem that comes down out of heaven from my God), and my new name as well.

¹³ Let the ones having ears hear what the Spirit says to the churches.'

[14] "*To the angel of the church in <u>Laodicea</u> write the following:*

"This is the solemn pronouncement of the Amen, the faithful and true witness, the originator of God's creation:
[15] 'I know your deeds, that you are neither cold nor hot. I wish you were either cold or hot! [16] So because you are lukewarm, and neither hot nor cold, I am going to vomit you out of my mouth!
[17] Because you say, "I am rich and have acquired great wealth, and need nothing," (but do not realize that you are wretched, pitiful, poor, blind, and naked!), [18] take my advice and buy gold from me refined by fire so you can become rich! Buy from me white clothing so you can be clothed and your shameful nakedness will not be exposed, and buy eye salve to put on your eyes so you can see!
[19] All those I love, I rebuke and discipline. So be earnest and repent! [20] Listen! I am standing at the door and knocking! If anyone hears my voice and opens the door I will come into his home and share a meal with him, and he with me. [21] I will grant the one who conquers permission to sit with me on my throne, just as I too conquered and sat down with my Father on his throne.
[22] Let the ones having ears hear what the Spirit says to the churches.'"

4:1 After these things I looked, and there was a door standing open in heaven! And the first voice I had heard speaking to me like a trumpet said: "*Come up here so that I can show you what must happen after these things.*"
[2] Immediately I was in the Spirit, and a throne was standing in heaven with someone seated on it! [3] And the one seated on it was like stones of jasper and carnelian in appearance, and a rainbow looking like it was made of emerald encircled the throne.

[4] In a circle around the throne were 24 other thrones, and seated on those thrones were 24 elders. They were dressed in white clothing and had golden crowns on their heads.

[5] From the throne came out flashes of lightning and roaring and crashes of thunder.

7 flaming torches, which are the 7 spirits of God, were burning in front of the throne [6] and in front of the throne was something like a sea of glass, like crystal.

In the middle of the throne and around the throne were 4 living creatures full of eyes in front and in back. [7] The first living creature was like a lion, the second creature like an ox, the third creature had a face like a man's, and the 4th creature looked like an eagle flying. [8] Each one of the 4 living creatures had 6 wings and was full of eyes all around and inside. They never rest day or night, saying:

> "*Holy Holy Holy is the Lord God,*
> *the All-Powerful,*
> *Who was*
> *and who is,*
> *and who is coming!*"

[9] And whenever the living creatures give glory, honor, and thanks to the one who sits on the throne, who lives forever and ever, [10] the 24 elders throw themselves to the ground before the one who sits on the throne and worship the one who lives forever and ever, and they offer their crowns before his throne, saying:

> [11] "*You are worthy, our Lord and God,*
> *to receive glory and honor and power,*
> *since you created all things,*
> *and because of your will they existed and were created!*"

5:1 Then I saw in the right hand of the one who was seated on the throne a scroll written on the front and back and sealed with 7 seals. [2] And I saw a powerful angel proclaiming in a loud voice:

"*Who is worthy to open the scroll and to break its seals?*"

[3] But no one in heaven or on earth or under the earth was able to open the scroll or look into it. [4] So I began weeping bitterly because no one was found who was worthy to open the scroll or to look into it.
    [5] Then one of the elders said to me,

"*Stop weeping!* ***Look***,
the Lion of the tribe of Judah,
 the root of David, has conquered;
thus he can open the scroll and its 7 seals."

[6] Then I ***saw*** standing in the middle of the throne and of the 4 living creatures, and in the middle of the elders, something like a slaughtered Lamb. He had 7 horns and 7 eyes, which are the 7 spirits of God sent out into all the earth.
    [7] Then he came and took the scroll from the right hand of the one who was seated on the throne, [8] and when he had taken the scroll, the 4 living creatures and the 24 elders threw themselves to the ground before the Lamb.
    Each of them had a harp and golden bowls full of incense, which are the prayers of the saints. [9] They were singing a new song:

"*You are worthy to take the scroll*
and to open its seals
because you were slaughtered,

and by your blood you ransomed for God
persons from every
　　tribe,
　　　language,
　　　　people,
　　　　　and nation!

[10] You have appointed them as a kingdom
and priests to serve our God,
and they will reign on the earth!"

[11] Then I looked and heard the voice of many angels in a circle around the throne, as well as the living creatures and the elders. Their number was 10,000 times 10,000– thousands times thousands– [12] all of whom were singing in a loud voice:

"*Worthy is the lamb who was slaughtered*
to receive power
　and wealth
　　and wisdom
　　　and might
　　　　and honor
　　　　　and glory
　　　　　　and praise!"

[13] Then I heard every creature– in heaven, on earth, under the earth, in the sea, and all that is in them– singing:

"*To the one seated on the throne and to the Lamb*
be praise,
　honor,
　　glory,
　　　and power
　　　　forever and ever!"

[14] And the 4 living creatures were saying "*Amen*," and the elders threw themselves to the ground and worshiped.

6:1 I looked when the Lamb opened one of the 7 seals, and I heard one of the 4 living creatures saying with a thunderous voice,

"*Come!*"

[2] So I looked, and behold, a white horse! The one who rode it had a bow, and he was given a crown, and as a conqueror he rode out to conquer.

[3] Then when the Lamb opened the 2nd seal, I heard the 2nd living creature saying,

"*Come!*"

[4] And another horse, fiery red, came out, and the one who rode it was granted permission to take peace from the earth, so that people would slaughter one another, and he was given a huge sword.

[5] Then when the Lamb opened the 3rd seal I heard the 3rd living creature saying,

"*Come!*"

So I looked, and here came a black horse! The one who rode it was holding balance scales in his hand. [6] Then I heard something like a voice from among the 4 living creatures saying,

"*A quart of wheat for a day's pay* (δηναρίου)
and 3 quarts of barley for a day's pay (δηναρίου).
But do not damage the olive oil and the wine!"

⁷ Then when the Lamb opened the 4ᵗʰ seal I heard the voice of the 4ᵗʰ living creature saying,

"Come!"

⁸ So I looked and here came a pale green horse! The name of the one who rode it was Death, and Hades followed right behind. They were given authority over a 4ᵗʰ of the earth, to kill its population with the sword, famine, and disease, and by the wild animals of the earth.

⁹ Now when the Lamb opened the 5ᵗʰ seal, I saw under the altar the souls of those who had been slaughtered on account of the word of God and on account of the testimony (μαρτυρίαν) they had given.
¹⁰ They cried out with a loud voice,

"How long, Sovereign Master, holy and true, before you judge
the ones living on the earth (τῶν κατοικούντων ἐπὶ τῆς γῆς)
and avenge our blood?"

¹¹ Each of them was given a long white robe and they were told to rest for a little longer, until the full number was reached of both their fellow servants and their brothers and sisters who were destined to be killed just as they had been.

¹² Then I looked when the Lamb opened the 6th seal, and a huge earthquake took place;
the sun became as black as sackcloth made of hair,
and the full moon became blood red;
¹³ and the stars in the sky fell to the earth
like a fig tree dropping its unripe figs when shaken by a fierce wind.
¹⁴ The sky was split apart like a scroll being rolled up,

and every mountain and island was moved from its place.

[15] Then the kings of the earth, the very important people, the generals, the rich, the powerful, and everyone, slave and free, hid themselves in the caves and among the rocks of the mountains. [16] They said to the mountains and to the rocks,

> "*Fall on us and hide us from the face of the one who is seated on the throne and from the wrath of the Lamb,*
> [17] *because the great day of their wrath has come, and who is able to stand?!*"

7:1 After this I saw 4 angels standing at the 4 corners of the earth, holding back the 4 winds of the earth so no wind could blow on the earth, on the sea, or on any tree.
[2] Then I saw another angel ascending from the east, who had the seal of the living God. He shouted out with a loud voice to the 4 angels who had been given permission to damage the earth and the sea:

> [3] "*Do not damage the earth or the sea or the trees until we have put a seal on the foreheads of the servants of our God.*"

[4] I **_heard_** the number of those who were marked with the seal, 144,000, sealed from all the tribes of the people of Israel:

[5] From the tribe of Judah,   12,000 having been sealed,
from the tribe of Reuben,   12,000,
from the tribe of Gad,   12,000,
[6] from the tribe of Asher,   12,000,
from the tribe of Naphtali,   12,000,
from the tribe of Manasseh,   12,000,

[7] from the tribe of Simeon,   12,000,
from the tribe of Levi,   12,000,
from the tribe of Issachar,   12,000,
[8] from the tribe of Zebulun,   12,000,
from the tribe of Joseph,   12,000,
from the tribe of Benjamin,   12,000
having been sealed.

[9] After these I **_looked_**, and behold, an enormous crowd that no one could count, made up of persons from every nation, tribe, people, and language, standing before the throne and before the Lamb dressed in long white robes, and with palm branches in their hands! [10] They were shouting out in a loud voice,

> "*Salvation belongs to our God,*
> *to the one seated on the throne,*
> *and to the Lamb!*"

[11] And all the angels stood there in a circle around the throne and around the elders and the 4 living creatures, and they threw themselves down with their faces to the ground before the throne and worshiped God, [12] saying,

> "*Amen! Praise and glory,*
> *and wisdom and thanksgiving,*
> *and honor and power and strength*
> *be to our God for ever and ever. Amen!*"

[13] Then one of the elders asked me,
> "*These dressed in long white robes–*
> *who are they and where have they come*
> *from?*"

[14] I said to him, "*My lord, you know.*"

Then he said to me,

"These are the ones who have come out of the great tribulation (θλίψεως). They have washed their robes and made them white in the blood of the Lamb!
[15] For this reason they are before the throne of God, and they serve him day and night in his temple, and the one seated on the throne will shelter them (σκηνώσει ἐπ' αὐτούς).
[16] They will never go hungry or be thirsty again, and the sun will not beat down on them, nor any burning heat, [17] because the Lamb in the middle of the throne will shepherd them and lead them to springs of living water, and God will wipe away every tear from their eyes."

8:1 Now when the Lamb opened the 7th seal there was silence in heaven for about half an hour.
[2] Then I saw the 7 angels who stand before God, and 7 trumpets were given to them. [3] Another angel holding a golden censer came and was stationed at the altar. A large amount of incense was given to him to offer up, with the prayers of all the saints, on the golden altar that is before the throne. [4] The smoke coming from the incense, along with the prayers of the saints, ascended before God from the angel's hand.
[5] Then the angel took the censer, filled it with fire from the altar, and threw it on the earth, and there were crashes of thunder, roaring, flashes of lightning, and an earthquake. [6] Now the 7 angels holding the 7 trumpets prepared to blow them.

[7] The 1st angel blew his trumpet, and there was hail and fire mixed with blood, and it was thrown at the earth so that a 3rd of the earth was burned up, a third of the trees were burned up, and all the green grass was burned up.

8 Then the 2nd angel blew his trumpet, and something like a great mountain of burning fire was thrown into the sea. A 3rd of the sea became blood, 9 and a third of the creatures living in the sea died, and a third of the ships were completely destroyed.

10 Then the 3rd angel blew his trumpet, and a huge star burning like a torch fell from the sky; it landed on a 3rd of the rivers and on the springs of water. 11 (Now the name of the star is Wormwood.) So a 3rd of the waters became wormwood, and many people died from these waters because they were poisoned.

12 Then the 4th angel blew his trumpet, and a 3rd of the sun was struck, and a 3rd of the moon, and a 3rd of the stars, so that a 3rd of them were darkened. And there was no light for a 3rd of the day and for a 3rd of the night likewise. 13 Then I looked, and I heard an eagle flying directly overhead, proclaiming with a loud voice, "*Woe! Woe! Woe to those who live on the earth because of the remaining sounds of the trumpets of the 3 angels who are about to blow them!*"

9:1 Then the 5th angel blew his trumpet, and I saw a star that had fallen from the sky to the earth, and he was given the key to the shaft of the abyss. 2 He opened the shaft of the abyss and smoke rose out of it like smoke from a giant furnace. The sun and the air were darkened with smoke from the shaft.
3 Then out of the smoke came locusts onto the earth, and they were given power like that of the scorpions of the earth. 4 They were told not to damage the grass of the earth, or any green plant or tree, but only those people who did not have the seal of God on their forehead. 5 The locusts were not given permission to kill them, but only to torture them for 5 months, and their torture was like that of a scorpion when it stings a person. 6 In those days people will seek death, but will

not be able to find it; they will long to die, but death will flee from them. [7] Now the locusts looked like horses equipped for battle. On their heads were something like crowns similar to gold, and their faces looked like men's faces. [8] They had hair like women's hair, and their teeth were like lions' teeth. [9] They had breastplates like iron breastplates, and the sound of their wings was like the noise of many horse-drawn chariots charging into battle. [10] They have tails and stingers like scorpions, and their ability to injure people for 5 months is in their tails. [11] They have as king over them the angel of the abyss, whose name in Hebrew is "Abaddon" (Destroyer), and in Greek, "Apollyon."

[12] The 1st woe has passed, but 2 woes are still coming after these things!

[13] Then the 6th angel blew his trumpet, and I heard a single voice coming from the horns on the golden altar that is before God, [14] saying to the 6th angel, the one holding the trumpet,

> "*Set free the 4 angels who are bound at the great river Euphrates!*"

[15] Then the 4 angels who had been prepared for this hour, day, month, and year were set free to kill a 3rd of humanity. [16] The number of soldiers on horseback was 200,000,000; I heard their number. [17] Now this is what the horses and their riders looked like in my vision: The riders had breastplates that were fiery red, dark blue, and sulfurous yellow in color. The heads of the horses looked like lions' heads, and fire, smoke, and sulfur came out of their mouths. [18] A 3rd of humanity was killed by these 3 plagues, that is, by the fire, the smoke, and the sulfur that came out of their mouths. [19] For the power of the horses resides in their mouths and in their tails, because their tails are like snakes, having heads that inflict injuries.

²⁰ The rest of humanity, who had not been killed by these plagues, did not repent of the works of their hands, so that they did not stop worshiping demons and idols made of gold, silver, bronze, stone, and wood– idols that cannot see or hear or walk about. ²¹ Furthermore, they did not repent of their murders, of their magic spells, of their sexual immorality, or of their stealing.

10:1 Then I saw another powerful angel descending from heaven, wrapped in a cloud, with a rainbow above his head; his face was like the sun and his legs were like pillars of fire. ² He held in his hand a little scroll that had been opened, and he put his right foot on the sea and his left on the land. ³ Then he shouted in a loud voice like a lion roaring, and when he shouted, the 7 thunders sounded their voices.

⁴ When the 7 thunders spoke, I was preparing to write, but just then I heard a voice from heaven say,

"Seal up what the 7 thunders spoke and do not write it down."

⁵ Then the angel I saw standing on the sea and on the land raised his right hand to heaven ⁶ and swore by the one who lives forever and ever, who created heaven and what is in it, and the earth and what is in it, and the sea and what is in it,

"There will be no more delay! ⁷ But in the days when the 7th angel is about to blow his trumpet, the mystery of God is completed, just as he has proclaimed to his servants the prophets."

⁸ Then the voice I had heard from heaven began to speak to me again,

"Go and take the open scroll in the hand of the angel who is standing on the sea and on the land."

[9] So I went to the angel and asked him to give me the little scroll. He said to me,

> *"Take the scroll and eat it. It will make your stomach bitter, but it will be as sweet as honey in your mouth."*

[10] So I took the little scroll from the angel's hand and ate it, and it did taste as sweet as honey in my mouth, but when I had eaten it, my stomach became bitter. [11] Then they told me:

> *"You must prophesy again about many peoples, nations, languages, and kings."*

11:1 Then a measuring rod like a staff was given to me, and I was told,

> *"Get up and measure the temple of God, and the altar, and the ones who worship there.* [2] *But do not measure the outer courtyard of the temple; leave it out, because it has been given to the Gentiles, and they will trample on the holy city for 42 months.* [3] *And I will grant my two witnesses authority to prophesy for 1,260 days, dressed in sackcloth."*

[4] These are the 2 olive trees and the 2 menorahs that stand before the Lord of the earth. [5] If anyone wants to harm them, fire comes out of their mouths and completely consumes their enemies. If anyone wants to harm them, they must be killed this way. [6] These 2 have the power to close up the sky so that it does not rain during the time they are prophesying. They have power to turn the waters to blood and to strike the earth with every kind of plague whenever they want.

[7] When they have completed their testimony, the beast that comes up from the abyss will make war

on them and conquer them and kill them. [8] Their corpses will lie in the street of the great city that is symbolically called Sodom and Egypt, where their Lord was also crucified. [9] For 3-and-a-half days those from every people, tribe, nation, and language will look at their corpses, because they will not permit them to be placed in a tomb. [10] And those who live on the earth will rejoice over them and celebrate, even sending gifts to each other, because these 2 prophets had tormented those who live on the earth (τοὺς κατοικοῦντας ἐπὶ τῆς γῆς).

[11] But after 3-and-a-half days a breath of life from God entered them, and they stood on their feet, and tremendous fear seized those who were watching them. [12] Then they heard a loud voice from heaven saying to them: "*Come up here!*" So the two prophets went up to heaven in a cloud while their enemies stared at them. [13] Just then a major earthquake took place and a 10th of the city collapsed; 7,000 people were killed in the earthquake, and the rest were terrified and gave glory to the God of heaven.

[14] The 2nd woe has come and gone; the 3rd is coming quickly (ταχύ).

[15] Then the 7th angel blew his trumpet, and there were loud voices in heaven saying:

> "*The kingdom of the world has become the kingdom of our Lord and of his Christ, and he will reign for ever and ever.*"

[16] Then the 24 elders who are seated on their thrones before God threw themselves down with their faces to the ground and worshiped God [17] with these words:

> "*We give you thanks, Lord God,*
> *the All-Powerful,*
> *the one who is*
> *and who was,*
> *because you have taken your great power*

and begun to reign.
[18] *The nations were enraged,*
but your wrath has come,
and the time has come for the dead to be
    judged,
and the time has come to give to your servants, the
prophets,
    their reward,
as well as to the saints and to those who revere
your name,
    both small and great,
and the time has come to destroy those who destroy
the earth!"

[19] Then the temple of God in heaven was opened and the ark of his covenant was visible within his temple. And there were flashes of lightning, roaring, crashes of thunder, an earthquake, and a great hailstorm.

12:1 Then a great sign appeared in heaven: a woman clothed with the sun, and with the moon under her feet, and on her head was a crown of 12 stars. [2] She was pregnant and was screaming in labor pains, struggling to give birth.

[3] Then another sign appeared in heaven: a huge red dragon that had 7 heads and 10 horns, and on its heads were 7 diadem crowns. [4] Now the dragon's tail swept away a 3rd of the stars in heaven and hurled them to the earth.

Then the dragon stood before the woman who was about to give birth, so that he might devour her child as soon as it was born. [5] So the woman gave birth to a son, a male child, who is going to rule over all the nations with an iron rod. Her child was suddenly caught up to God and to his throne, [6] and she fled into the wilderness where a place had been prepared for her by God, so she could be taken care of for 1,260 days.

[7] Then war broke out in heaven: Michael and his angels fought against the dragon, and the dragon

and his angels fought back. ⁸ But the dragon was not strong enough to prevail, so there was no longer any place left in heaven for him and his angels. ⁹ So that huge dragon– the ancient serpent, the one called the devil and Satan, who deceives the whole world– was thrown down to the earth, and his angels along with him.

¹⁰ Then I heard a loud voice in heaven saying,

> "The salvation and the power and the kingdom of our God, and the ruling authority of his Messiah, have now come, because the accuser of our brothers and sisters, the one who accuses them day and night before our God, has been cast down.
>   ¹¹ But they overcame him by the blood of the Lamb and by the word of their testimony, and they did not love their lives even unto death. ¹² Therefore you heavens rejoice, and all who reside in them!
>   But woe to the earth and the sea because the devil has come down to you! He is filled with terrible anger, for he knows that he only has a little time!"

¹³ Now when the dragon realized that he had been thrown down to the earth, he pursued the woman who had given birth to the male child. ¹⁴ But the woman was given the two wings of a giant eagle so that she could fly out into the wilderness, to the place God prepared for her, where she is taken care of– away from the presence of the serpent–

for a time,
    times,
        and half a time.

¹⁵ Then the serpent spewed water like a river out of his mouth after the woman in order to sweep her away by a flood, ¹⁶ but the earth came to her rescue; the ground opened up and swallowed the river that the dragon had spewed from his mouth. ¹⁷ So the dragon became

184

enraged at the woman and went away to make war on the rest of her children, those who keep God's commandments and hold to the testimony about Jesus.

¹⁸ And the dragon stood on the sand of the seashore. **13:1** Then I saw a beast coming up out of the sea. It had 10 horns and 7 heads, and on its horns were 10 diadem crowns, and on its heads a blasphemous name. ² Now the beast that I saw was like a leopard, but its feet were like a bear's, and its mouth was like a lion's mouth.

The dragon gave the beast his power, his throne, and great authority to rule. ³ One of the beast's heads looked as if it had been slaughtered to death, but the death wound had been healed. And the whole world followed the beast in amazement; ⁴ they worshiped the dragon because he had given ruling authority to the beast, and they worshiped the beast too, saying:

"Who is like the beast?"

and

"Who is able to make war against him?"

⁵ The beast was given a mouth speaking proud words and blasphemies, and he was permitted to exercise ruling authority for 42 months. ⁶ So the beast opened his mouth to blaspheme against God– to blaspheme both his name and his dwelling place, that is, those who dwell in heaven (τοὺς ἐν τῷ οὐρανῷ σκηνοῦντας). ⁷ The beast was permitted to go to war against the saints and conquer them. He was given ruling authority over every tribe, people, language, and nation, ⁸ and all those who live on the earth (οἱ κατοικοῦντες ἐπὶ τῆς γῆς) will worship the beast, everyone whose name has not been written in the book of life belonging to the Lamb who was slaughtered from the foundation of the world.

[or: "everyone whose name has not been written in the book of life since the foundation of the world belonging to the Lamb who was slaughtered."]

[9] If anyone has an ear, he had better listen!
[10] If anyone is meant for captivity,
        into captivity he will go.
If anyone is to be killed by the sword,
        then by the sword he must be killed.
This requires steadfast endurance and faith from the saints.

[11] Then I saw another beast coming up from the earth. He had 2 horns like a lamb, but was speaking like a dragon. [12] He exercised all the ruling authority of the 1st beast on his behalf, and made the earth and those who inhabit it (κατοικοῦντας) worship the 1st beast, the one whose death wound had been healed.
[13] He performed momentous signs, even making fire come down from heaven in front of people [14] and, by the signs he was permitted to perform on behalf of the beast, he deceived those who live on the earth (τοὺς κατοικοῦντας ἐπὶ τῆς γῆς). He told those who live on the earth (τοῖς κατοικοῦσιν ἐπὶ τῆς γῆς) to make an image to the beast who had been wounded by the sword but still lived. [15] The 2nd beast was empowered to give life to the image of the 1st beast so that it could speak, and could cause all those who did not worship the image of the beast to be killed.
[16] He also caused everyone (small and great, rich and poor, free and slave) to obtain a mark on their right hand or on their forehead. [17] Thus no one was allowed to buy or sell things unless he bore the mark of the beast– that is, his name or his number. [18] This calls for wisdom: Let the one who has insight calculate the beast's number, for it is man's number, and his number is 666.

14:1 Then I looked, and here was the Lamb standing on Mount Zion, and with him were 144,000, who had his name and his Father's name written on their foreheads. [2] I also heard a sound coming out of heaven like the sound of many waters and like the sound of loud thunder. Now the sound I heard was like that made by harpists playing their harps, [3] and they were singing a new song before the throne and before the 4 living creatures and the elders. No one was able to learn the song except the 144,000 who had been redeemed from the earth.

[4] These are the ones who have not defiled themselves with women,

> for they are virgins.

These are the ones who follow the Lamb wherever he goes.

These were redeemed from humanity as firstfruits to God and to the

> Lamb,
> [5] and no lie was found on their lips;
> they are blameless.

[6] Then I saw another angel flying directly overhead, and he had an eternal gospel (εὐαγγέλιον) to proclaim to those who live on the earth– to every nation, tribe, language, and people. [7] He declared in a loud voice:

> *"Fear God and give him glory, because the hour of his judgment has arrived, and worship the one who made heaven and earth, the sea and the springs of water!"*

[8] A 2nd angel followed the 1st, declaring:

> *"Fallen, fallen is Babylon the great city!*
> *She made all the nations drink of the wine of her immoral passion."*

[9] A 3rd angel followed the first 2, declaring in a loud voice:

> "*If anyone worships the beast and his image, and takes the mark on his forehead or his hand, [10] that person will also drink of the wine of God's anger that has been mixed undiluted in the cup of his wrath, and he will be tortured with fire and sulfur in front of the holy angels and in front of the Lamb. [11] And the smoke from their torture will go up forever and ever, and those who worship the beast and his image will have no rest day or night, along with anyone who receives the mark of his name.*"

[12] This requires the steadfast endurance of the saints-- those who obey God's commandments and hold to their faith in Jesus.

[13] Then I heard a voice from heaven say,

> "*Write this:*
> *'Blessed are the dead, those who die in the*
> *   Lord*
> *from this moment on [or 'assuredly!']'*"
> "*Yes,*" *says the Spirit,* "*so they can rest*
> *   from their hard work,*
> *   because their deeds will follow them.*"

[14] Then I looked, and a white cloud appeared, and seated on the cloud was one like a Son of Man! He had a golden crown on his head and a sharp sickle in his hand. [15] Then another angel came out of the temple, shouting in a loud voice to the one seated on the cloud,

> "*Use your sickle and start to reap,*
> *because the time to reap has come,*
> *since the earth's harvest is ripe!*"

[16] So the one seated on the cloud swung his sickle over the earth, and the earth was reaped.

[17] Then another angel came out of the temple in heaven, and he too had a sharp sickle. [18] Another angel, who was in charge of the fire, came from the altar and called in a loud voice to the angel who had the sharp sickle,

> *"Use your sharp sickle and gather the clusters of grapes off the vine of the earth, because its grapes are now ripe."*

[19] So the angel swung his sickle over the earth and gathered the grapes from the vineyard of the earth and tossed them into the great winepress of the wrath of God. [20] Then the winepress was stomped outside the city, and blood poured out of the winepress up to the height of horses' bridles for a distance of almost 200 miles (1,600 stadia).

15:1 Then I saw another great and astounding sign in heaven: 7 angels who have 7 final plagues (they are final because in them God's anger is completed). [2] Then I saw something like a sea of glass mixed with fire, and those who had conquered (νικῶντας) the beast and his image and the number of his name. They were standing by the sea of glass, holding harps given to them by God. [3] They sang the song of Moses the servant of God and the song of the Lamb:

> *"Great and astounding are your deeds,*
> *Lord God, the All-Powerful!*
> *Just and true are your ways,*
> *King over the nations!*
> [4] *Who will not fear you, O Lord,*
> *and glorify your name,*
> *because you alone are holy?*

> *All nations will come and worship before you*
> > *for your righteous acts have been revealed.*"

[5] After these things I looked, and the temple—the tent of the testimony—was opened in heaven, [6] and the 7 angels who had the 7 plagues came out of the temple, dressed in clean bright linen, wearing wide golden belts around their chests. [7] Then one of the 4 living creatures gave the 7 angels 7 golden bowls filled with the wrath of God who lives forever and ever, [8] and the temple was filled with smoke from God's glory and from his power. Thus no one could enter the temple until the 7 plagues from the 7 angels were completed.

16:1 Then I heard a loud voice from the temple declaring to the 7 angels:
> "*Go and pour out on the earth the 7 bowls containing God's wrath.*"

[2] So the 1st angel went and poured out his bowl on the earth. Then ugly and painful sores appeared on the people who had the mark of the beast and who worshiped his image.

[3] Next, the 2nd angel poured out his bowl on the sea and it turned into blood, like that of a corpse, and every living creature that was in the sea died.

[4] Then the 3rd angel poured out his bowl on the rivers and the springs of water, and they turned into blood. [5] Now I heard the angel of the waters saying:

> "*You are just–*
> > *the one who is*
> > > *and who was,*
> > > > *the Holy One–*

> *because you have passed these judgments,*
> [6] *because they poured out the blood of your*

190

> saints and prophets,
> so you have given them blood to drink.
> They got what they deserved!"

⁷ Then I heard the altar reply,

> "Yes, Lord God, the All-Powerful,
> your judgments are true and just!"

⁸ Then the 4th angel poured out his bowl on the sun, and it was permitted to scorch people with fire. ⁹ Thus people were scorched by the terrible heat, yet they blasphemed the name of God, who has ruling authority over these plagues, and they would not repent and give him glory.

¹⁰ Then the 5ᵗʰ angel poured out his bowl on the throne of the beast so that darkness covered his kingdom, and people began to bite their tongues because of their pain. ¹¹ They blasphemed the God of heaven because of their sufferings and because of their sores, but nevertheless they still refused to repent of their deeds.

¹² Then the 6th angel poured out his bowl on the great river Euphrates and dried up its water to prepare the way for the kings from the east. ¹³ Then I saw 3 unclean spirits that looked like frogs coming out of the mouth of the dragon, out of the mouth of the beast, and out of the mouth of the false prophet. ¹⁴ For they are the spirits of the demons performing signs who go out to the kings of the earth to bring them together for the battle that will take place on the great day of God, the All-Powerful.

> ¹⁵ (Look! I will come like a thief! Blessed is the one keeping watch and guarding his garments so that he will not have to walk around naked and his shameful condition be seen.)

¹⁶ Now the spirits gathered the kings and their armies to the place that is called "Armageddon"

(Ἀρμαγεδών = הַרְמְגִדּוֹן) in Hebrew.

¹⁷ Finally the 7th angel poured out his bowl into the air and a loud voice came out of the temple from the throne, saying:

"It is done!"

¹⁸ Then there were flashes of lightning, roaring, and crashes of thunder, and there was a tremendous earthquake– an earthquake unequaled since humanity has been on the earth, so tremendous was that earthquake. ¹⁹ The great city was split into 3 parts and the cities of the nations collapsed.

So Babylon the great was remembered before God, and was given the cup filled with the wine made of God's furious wrath.

²⁰ Every island fled away and no mountains could be found. ²¹ And gigantic hailstones, weighing about a hundred pounds each, fell from heaven on people, but they blasphemed God because of the plague of hail, since it was so horrendous.

17:1 Then one of the 7 angels who had the 7 bowls came and spoke to me.

"Come," he said, *"I will show you the condemnation and punishment of the great prostitute who sits on many waters,* ² *with whom the kings of the earth committed sexual immorality and the inhabitants of the earth* (οἱ κατοικοῦντες τὴν γῆν) *got drunk with the wine of her immorality."*

³ So he carried me away in the Spirit to a wilderness, and there I saw a woman sitting on a scarlet beast that was full of blasphemous names and had 7 heads and 10 horns. ⁴ Now the woman was dressed in purple and scarlet clothing, and adorned with gold, precious

stones, and pearls. She held in her hand a golden cup filled with detestable things and unclean things from her sexual immorality. [5] On her forehead was written a name, a mystery:

> **BABYLON THE GREAT, THE MOTHER OF PROSTITUTES**
> **AND OF THE DETESTABLE THINGS OF THE EARTH**

[6] I saw that the woman was drunk with the blood of the saints and the blood of those who testified (τῶν μαρτύρων) to Jesus.

I was greatly astounded when I saw her. [7] But the angel said to me,

> *"Why are you astounded? I will interpret for you the mystery of the woman and of the beast with the 7 heads and 10 horns that carries her.*
> [8] *The beast you saw*
> > *was,*
> > > *and is not,*
> > > > *but is about to come*
> *up from the abyss and then go to destruction.*
> *The inhabitants of the earth* (οἱ κατοικοῦντες ἐπὶ τῆς γῆς)—*all those whose names have not been written in the book of life since the foundation of the world– will be astounded when they see that the beast*
> > *was,*
> > > *and is not,*
> > > > *but is to come.*

[9] (This requires a mind that has wisdom.)

> *The 7 heads are 7 mountains the woman sits on. They are also 7 kings:*

^{10} *5 have fallen;*
   one is,
      and the other has not yet come,

but whenever he does come, he must remain for only a brief time.

      ^{11} *The beast*
         that was,
            and is not,
      is himself an 8th king
         and yet is one of the 7,
            and is going to destruction.

^{12} *The 10 horns that you saw are 10 kings who have not yet received a kingdom, but will receive ruling authority as kings with the beast for one hour.* ^{13} *These kings have a single intent, and they will give their power and authority to the beast.*
      ^{14} *They will make war with the Lamb, but the Lamb will conquer them, because he is Lord of lords and King of kings, and those accompanying the Lamb are the called, chosen, and faithful."*

^{15} Then the angel said to me,

      "*The waters you saw (where the prostitute is seated) are peoples, multitudes, nations, and languages.*
      ^{16} *The 10 horns that you saw, and the beast– these will hate the prostitute and make her desolate and naked. They will consume*
         her flesh and burn her up with fire. ^{17} *For God has put into their minds to carry out his purpose by making a decision to give their royal power to the beast until the words of God are fulfilled.*

¹⁸ *As for the woman you saw, she is the great city that has sovereignty over the kings of the earth."*

18:1 After these things I saw another angel, who possessed great authority, coming down out of heaven, and the earth was lit up by his radiance. ² He shouted with a powerful voice:

"Fallen, fallen, is Babylon the great!
She has become a lair for demons,
  a haunt for every unclean spirit,
  a haunt for every unclean bird,
  a haunt for every unclean and detested beast.
³ *For all the nations have fallen from the wine of her immoral passion, and the kings of the earth have committed sexual immorality with her, and the merchants of the earth have gotten rich from the power of her sensual behavior."*

⁴ Then I heard another voice from heaven saying,

"Come out of her, my people, so you will not take part in her sins and so you will not receive her plagues, ⁵ because her sins have piled up all the way to heaven and God has remembered her crimes.
  ⁶ *Repay her the same way she repaid others; pay her back double corresponding to her deeds. In the cup she mixed, mix double the amount for her. ⁷ As much as she exalted herself and lived in sensual luxury, to this extentt give her torment and grief because she said to herself,*
    'I rule as queen and am no widow;
    I will never experience grief!'
⁸ *For this reason, she will experience her plagues in a single day: disease, mourning,*

and famine, and she will be burned down with
fire, because the Lord God who judges her is
powerful!"

[9] Then the kings of the earth who committed immoral acts with her and lived in sensual luxury with her will weep and wail for her when they see the smoke from the fire that burns her up. [10] They will stand a long way off because they are afraid of her torment, and will say,

"Woe, woe, O great city,
Babylon the powerful city!
For in a single hour your doom has come!"

[11] Then the merchants of the earth will weep and mourn for her because no one buys their cargo any longer– [12] cargo such as gold, silver, precious stones, pearls, fine linen, purple cloth, silk, scarlet cloth, all sorts of things made of citron wood, all sorts of objects made of ivory, all sorts of things made of expensive wood, bronze, iron and marble, [13] cinnamon, spice, incense, perfumed ointment, frankincense, wine, olive oil and costly flour, wheat, cattle and sheep, horses and 4-wheeled carriages, slaves and human lives. [14] (The ripe fruit you greatly desired has gone from you, and all your luxury and splendor have gone from you– they will never ever be found again!)
[15] The merchants who sold these things, who got rich from her, will stand a long way off because they are afraid of her torment. They will weep and mourn, [16] saying,

"Woe, woe, O great city–
dressed in fine linen, purple and scarlet
clothing,
and adorned with gold, precious stones, and
pearls–
[17] *because in a single hour such great wealth*
has been destroyed!"

And every ship's captain, and all who sail along the coast– seamen, and all who make their living from the sea, stood a long way off [18] and began to shout when they saw the smoke from the fire that burned her up,

> "*Who is like the great city?*"

[19] And they threw dust on their heads and were shouting with weeping and mourning,

> "*Woe, Woe, O great city–*
> *in which all those who had ships on the sea*
> *got rich from her wealth–*
> *because in a single hour she has been destroyed!*"

[20] (Rejoice over her, O heaven, and you saints and apostles and prophets, for God has pronounced judgment against her on your behalf!)

[21] Then one powerful angel picked up a stone like a huge millstone, threw it into the sea, and said,

> "*With this kind of sudden violent force Babylon the great city will be thrown down and it will never be found again!*
> [22] *And the sound of the harpists, musicians, flute players, and trumpeters will never be heard in you again.*
> *No craftsman who practices any trade will ever be found in you again; the noise of a mill will never be heard in you again.*
> [23] *Even the light from a lamp will never shine in you again!*
> *The voices of the bridegroom and his bride will never be heard in you again.*
> *For your merchants were the tycoons of the world, because all the nations were deceived by your magic spells!* [24] *The blood of*

*the saints and prophets was found in her,
along with the blood of all those who had been
killed on the earth."*

19:1 After these things I heard what sounded like the loud voice of a vast throng in heaven, saying,

*"Hallelujah!
Salvation and glory and power belong to our
    God,
[2] because his judgments are true and just.
For he has judged the great prostitute
    who corrupted the earth with her sexual
        immorality,
and has avenged the blood of his servants
    poured out by her own hands!"*

[3] Then a second time the crowd shouted,

"Hallelujah!"

The smoke rises from her forever and ever. [4] The 24 elders and the 4 living creatures threw themselves to the ground and worshiped God, who was seated on the throne, saying:

"Amen! Hallelujah!"

[5] Then a voice came from the throne, saying:

*"Praise our God all you his servants,
and all you who fear Him,
both the small and the great!"*

[6] Then I heard what sounded like the voice of a vast throng, like the roar of many waters and like loud crashes of thunder. They were shouting:

*"Hallelujah!
For the Lord our God, the All-Powerful, reigns!*

⁷ Let us rejoice and exult and give him glory,
   because the wedding celebration of the Lamb has come,
    and his bride has made herself ready.
⁸ She was permitted to be dressed in bright, clean, fine linen"
(for the fine linen is the righteous deeds of the saints).

⁹ Then the angel **_said_** to me,

> *"Write the following:*
> *Blessed are those who are invited to the banquet*
> *at the wedding celebration of the Lamb!"*

He also said to me,

> *"These are the true words of God."*

¹⁰ So I threw myself down at his feet to worship him, but he said,

> *"Do not do this! I am only a fellow servant with you and your brothers who hold to the testimony about Jesus. Worship God, for the testimony (μαρτυρίαν) of Jesus is the spirit of prophecy."*

¹¹ Then I **_saw_** heaven opened and here came a white horse! The one riding it was called "FAITHFUL" and "TRUE," and with justice he judges and goes to war.
¹² His eyes are like a fiery flame and there are many diadem crowns on his head.
He has a name written that no one knows except himself.
¹³ He is dressed in clothing dipped in blood, and he is called the Word of God.

¹⁴ The armies that are in heaven, dressed in white, clean, fine linen, were following him on white horses. ¹⁵ From his mouth extends a sharp sword, so that with it he can strike the nations.

He will rule them with an iron rod, and he stomps the winepress of the furious wrath of God, the All-Powerful. ¹⁶ He has a name written on his clothing and on his thigh:

KING OF KINGS AND LORD OF LORDS

¹⁷ Then I saw one angel standing in the sun, and he shouted in a loud voice to all the birds flying high in the sky:

> "*Come, gather around*
> *for the great banquet of God,*
> ¹⁸ *to eat your fill of the flesh of kings,*
> *the flesh of generals,*
> *the flesh of powerful people,*
> *the flesh of horses*
> *and those who ride them,*
> *and the flesh of all people,*
> *both free and slave,*
> *and small and great!*"

¹⁹ Then I saw the beast and the kings of the earth and their armies assembled to do battle with the one who rode the horse and with his army. ²⁰ Now the beast was seized, and along with him the false prophet who had performed the signs on his behalf– signs by which he deceived those who had received the mark of the beast and those who worshiped his image. Both of them were thrown alive into the lake of fire burning with sulfur. ²¹ The others were killed by the sword that extended from the mouth of the one who rode the

horse, and all the birds gorged themselves with their flesh.

20:1 Then I saw an angel descending from heaven, holding in his hand the key to the abyss and a huge chain. [2] He seized the dragon– the ancient serpent, who is the devil and Satan– and bound him for 1,000 years. [3] The angel then threw him into the abyss and locked and sealed it so that he could not deceive the nations until the 1,000 years were finished.

(After these things (μετὰ ταῦτα) he must be released for a brief period of time.)

[4] Then I saw thrones and seated on them were those who had been given authority to judge.

I also saw the souls of those who had been beheaded because of the testimony (μαρτυρίαν) of Jesus and because of the word of God. These had not worshiped the beast or his image and had refused to receive his mark on their forehead or hand. They came to life and reigned with Christ for 1,000 years.

[5] (The rest of the dead did not come to life until the thousand years were finished.)

This is the first resurrection. [6] Blessed and holy is the one who takes part in the first resurrection. The second death has no power over them, but they will be priests of God and of Christ, and they will reign with him for 1,000 years.

[7] Now when the 1,000 years are finished, Satan will be released from his prison [8] and will go out to deceive the nations at the 4 corners of the earth, Gog and Magog, to bring them together for the battle. They are as numerous as the grains of sand in the sea.

[9] They went up on the broad plain of the earth and encircled the camp of the saints and the beloved city, but fire came down from heaven and devoured them completely.

[10] And the devil who deceived them was thrown into the lake of fire and sulfur, where the beast

and the false prophet are too, and they will be tormented there day and night forever and ever.

[11] Then I saw a large white throne and the one who was seated on it; the earth and the heaven fled from his presence, and no place was found for them. [12] And I saw the dead, the great and the small, standing before the throne. Then books were opened, and another book was opened– the book of life. So the dead were judged by what was written in the books, according to their deeds. [13] The sea gave up the dead that were in it, and Death and Hades gave up the dead that were in them, and each one was judged according to his deeds.

[14] Then Death and Hades were thrown into the lake of fire.

This is the second death– the lake of fire. [15] If anyone's name was not found written in the book of life, that person was thrown into the lake of fire.

21:1 Then I saw a new heaven and a new earth, for the 1st heaven and earth had gone away, and the sea was no more. [2] And I saw the holy city– the new Jerusalem– descending out of heaven from God, made ready like a bride adorned for her husband. [3] And I heard a loud voice from the throne saying:

"Look! The residence (σκηνὴ) of God is among human beings.

He will live (σκηνώσει) among them,
and they will be his people,
and God himself will be with them.

[4] He will wipe away every tear from their eyes,
and death will not exist any more–
  or mourning,
  or crying,
  or pain,
for the former things have gone away."

⁵ And the one seated on the throne said:

> "*Look! I am making all things new!*"

Then he said to me,

> "*Write it down, because these words are reliable and true.*"

⁶ He also said to me,

> "*It is done!*
> *I am the Alpha and the Omega,*
> *the beginning and the end.*
> *To the one who is thirsty I will give water free of charge from the spring of the water of life.* ⁷ *The one who conquers* (ὁ νικῶν) *will inherit these things, and I will be his God and he will be my son.* ⁸ *But to the cowards, unbelievers, detestable persons, murderers, the sexually immoral, and those who practice magic spells, idol worshipers, and all those who lie, their place will be in the lake that burns with fire and sulfur. That is the second death.*"

⁹ Then one of the 7 angels who had the 7 bowls full of the 7 final plagues came and spoke to me, saying,

> "*Come, I will show you the bride, the wife of the Lamb!*"

¹⁰ So he took me away in the Spirit to a huge, majestic mountain and showed me the holy city, Jerusalem, descending out of heaven from God. ¹¹ The city possesses the glory of God; its brilliance is like a precious jewel, like a stone of crystal-clear jasper.

[12] It has a massive, high wall with 12 gates, with 12 angels at the gates, and the names of the 12 tribes of the nation of Israel are written on the gates.

[13] There are 3 gates on the east side, 3 gates on the north side, 3 gates on the south side and 3 gates on the west side.

[14] The wall of the city has 12 foundations, and on them are the 12 names of the 12 apostles of the Lamb.

[15] The angel who spoke to me had a golden measuring rod with which to measure the city and its foundation stones and wall.

[16] Now the city is laid out as a square, its length and width the same. He measured the city with the measuring rod at 14,000 miles (12,000 σταδίων) (its length and width and height are equal).

[17] He also measured its wall, about 216 feet (144 cubits) according to human measurement, which is also the angel's. [18] The city's wall is made of jasper and the city is pure gold, like transparent glass. [19] The foundations of the city's wall are decorated with every kind of precious stone.

The 1st foundation is jasper,
the 2nd sapphire,
the 3rd agate,
the 4th emerald,
[20] the 5th onyx,
the 6th carnelian,
the 7th chrysolite,
the 8th beryl,
the 9th topaz,
the 10th chrysoprase,
the 11th jacinth,
and the 12th amethyst.

[21] And the 12 gates are 12 pearls—
each one of the gates is made from just one pearl!
The main street of the city is pure gold,
like transparent glass.

[22] Now I saw no temple in the city, because the Lord God– the All-Powerful– and the Lamb are its temple.

[23] The city does not need the sun or the moon to shine on it, because the glory of God lights it up, and its lamp is the Lamb. [24] The nations will walk by its light and the kings of the earth will bring their grandeur into it. [25] Its gates will never be closed during the day (and there will be no night there). [26] They will bring the grandeur and the wealth of the nations into it, [27] but nothing ritually unclean will ever enter into it, nor anyone who does what is detestable or practices falsehood, but only those whose names are written in the Lamb's book of life.

22:1 Then the angel showed me the river of the water of life– water as clear as crystal– pouring out from the throne of God and of the Lamb, [2] flowing down the middle of the city's main street.

On each side of the river is the tree of life producing 12 kinds of fruit, yielding its fruit every month of the year. Its leaves are for the healing of the nations. [3] And there will no longer be any curse, and the throne of God and the Lamb will be in the city. His servants will worship him, [4] and they will see his face, and his name will be on their foreheads.

[5] Night will be no more, and they will not need the light of a lamp or the light of the sun, because the Lord God will shine on them, and they will reign forever and ever.

[6] Then the angel said to me,

> *"These words are reliable and true. The Lord, the God of the spirits of the prophets, has sent his angel to show his servants what must happen soon.*
> [7] *Look! I am coming soon!*
> *Blessed is the one who keeps the words of the prophecy of this book."*

⁸ I, John, am the one who heard and saw these things, and when I heard and saw them, I threw myself down to worship at the feet of the angel who was showing them to me. ⁹ But he said to me,

> "*Do not do this! I am a fellow servant with you and with your brothers the prophets, and with those who obey the words of this book. Worship God!*"

¹⁰ Then he said to me,

> "*Do not seal up the words of the prophecy contained in this book, because the time is near.*
> ¹¹ *The evildoer must continue to do evil, and the one who is morally filthy must continue to be filthy. The one who is righteous must continue to act righteously, and the one who is holy must continue to be holy.*"

¹² *Look! I am coming soon, and my reward is with me to pay each one according to what he has done!*

¹³ *I am the Alpha and the Omega,
the first and the last,
the beginning and the end!*

¹⁴ *Blessed are those who wash their robes so they can have access to the tree of life and can enter into the city by the gates.*
¹⁵ *Outside are the dogs and the sorcerers and the sexually immoral, and the murderers, and the idolaters and everyone who loves and practices falsehood!*

¹⁶ *I, Jesus, have sent my angel to testify to you about these things for the churches.*

I am the root and the descendant of David,
    the bright morning star!
¹⁷ And the Spirit and the bride say,
    'Come!'
And let the one who hears say:
    'Come!'
And let the one who is thirsty come;
let the one who wants it take the water of life
    free of charge.

¹⁸ I testify (Μαρτυρῶ ἐγὼ) to the one who hears the words of the prophecy contained in this book:

If anyone adds to them, God will add to him the plagues described in this book.

¹⁹ And if anyone takes away from the words of this book of prophecy, God will take away his share in the tree of life and in the holy city that are described in this book.

²⁰ The one who testifies (ὁ μαρτυρῶν) to these things says,

    'Yes, I am coming swiftly/soon (ταχύ)!'"

Amen! Come, Lord Jesus!

²¹ The grace of the Lord Jesus be with all.

-Appendix C-
The 144,000: An Exegetical Look at Revelation 14:1-5

Text:

14:1 *I looked and behold, the lamb was standing on Mt. Zion and with him were the 144,000 with his name and the name of his Father having been written on their foreheads. 2And I heard a sound from heaven that was like the sound of many waters and like the sound of great thunder. This sound that I heard was like the sound of harpists harping on their harps. 3And they sing a new song before the throne and before the four living ones and the elders, and no one was able to understand the song except the 144,000 who have been purchased from the earth. 4These are the ones who had not been defiled with women, for they are celibates. These are the ones following the lamb wherever he goes. These were purchased from humanity as firstfruits to God and the lamb. 5And in their mouth no lie was found; they are unblemished.*

Literary Setting:

Immediately prior to this passage, John has been given a vision that depicts the rise of the unholy trinity (The Dragon, the Sea Beast, and the Land Beast) and their subsequent assault on the church in chapters 12 and 13. The forces of evil were able to conquer and kill anyone who remained loyal to God and refused to take the mark of the Sea Beast. Despite having been sealed in chapter 7, the believers were allowed to suffer physically. In fact, they were told, almost nonchalantly, that if they were to be taken captive, into captivity they would go; if they were to be slain with the sword, with the sword they would be slain (13:10). This was a call for endurance on the part of God's people. But why should they have to endure this? What would be their reward?

It is precisely that question that is answered in chapter 14. And in the first five verses, John sees a vision of the reward of the faithful. As Mounce states: "The detailed description of the beast and the false prophet in the preceding chapter was a somber reminder of what lay ahead in the immediate future. A note of encouragement is in order."[30] While

---

[30] Mounce, Robert H. The Book of Revelation: NICNT. Eerdmans, Grand Rapids. 1977, p. 266

scholars disagree as to when exactly the celebration in vv. 1-5 are to set to take place, for John's readers, the chronology is not as important as the actual content of the vision. As Wall notes:

> According to their cosmology, shaped by Platonic thought, what happens in heaven determines what happens on earth. In this sense, the future period of salvation's history has already been determined by what has already transpired in the heavenly realm: the "eternal gospel" is not that God will triumph at some point in the indefinite future; but that God has already triumphed through the Risen Christ in the definite past.[31]

John's readers are given the promise of joyous celebration that is to be theirs in direct contrast to the tyrannical reign of the Dragon and the Beasts over the "earth dwellers" (τοὺς καθημένους ἐπὶ τῆς γῆς), a term John uses to refer to unbelievers. Noting this, Wall feels that every part of John's account in 14:1-5 is a deliberate contrast to the reign of evil in chapter 13--oppression has been exchanged for liberation, evil for good, suffering for celebration: "By using contrasting images,

---

[31] Wall, Robert W. <u>Revelation: NIBC</u>. Hendrickson, Peabody. 1991, p.177.

John invites the rhetorical question—for whom is this experience of liberation a reality?"[32]

Commentary

V.1) The first thing that John beholds is the Lamb standing on Mt. Zion along with the 144,000 saints who had been sealed with God's mark on their foreheads in chapter 7. The fact that they are standing on Mt. Zion seems to argue for an eschatological gathering of God's people. Though Mt. Zion referred to the present reality of the kingdom of God in Hebrews 12:22, the OT, John's primary source of imagery in Revelation, spoke of Mt. Zion as an end-time sanctuary for Israel. "*Then the LORD will create over the whole site of Mount Zion and over her assemblies a cloud by day, and smoke and the shining of a flaming fire by night; for over all the glory there will be a canopy (Isa 4:5).*" Not only would Israel finally be safe, YHWH Himself would dwell with them: "*And it shall come to pass that everyone who calls on the name of the LORD shall be saved. For in Mount Zion and in Jerusalem there shall be those who escape, as the LORD has said, and among the survivors shall be those whom the LORD calls (Joel 2:32).*" The concept of the Messiah gathering God's

---

[32] Ibid 178.

people on Mt. Zion is even found in extra-biblical Jewish writings. According to Beale, 4 Ezra 13:25-32 and 2 Bar 40 speak of the "Son" and "Messiah" standing on "Mount Zion" at the end time judging the unrighteous and "defending" or "protecting" the remnant.[33] Therefore, it is most likely that v.1 is depicting the final confrontation between the people of God and the ungodly nations that will take place at the end of history.

Aside from the issue of this passage's chronology, there is the issue of this passage's geography. Is the celebration on Mt. Zion located in heaven or on earth? Scholars are divided on this issue.[34] Beale feels that the presence of the Lamb supports a Heavenly Zion due to the fact that all of John's other references to the Lamb place him in heaven.[35] However, in light of the OT prophecies regarding Mt. Zion, an earthly locale is not out of the question. Wall argues, probably correctly, that John is using a geographical reference as a theological idiom. "His use of Mount Zion probably refers here to the historical and eschatological (rather than a spiritual and existential) fulfillment of God's

---

[33] Beale, G.K. Revelation: NIGTC. Eerdmans, Grand Rapids. 1999, p.732
[34] Osborne, Beale, Mounce, and Morris see it as a heavenly vision while Aune, Johnson, and Ladd see it as an earthly event at the actual Mt. Zion.
[35] Beal 732

212

promised restoration of true Israel."[36] Though Mt. Zion is seen in John's vision as a geographical setting, it is symbolic of a theological truth that believers in John's day can appreciate—those who are sealed by God will stand with him in triumph and safety as the nations are judged.

As noted above, the 144,000 in this verse are the 144,000 from the tribes of Israel who were sealed in chapter 7. The fact that they are from the tribes of Israel doesn't mean that they are ethnic Jews or that their number is literally 144,000. In chapter 7 immediately after John heard their number and their tribes he turn and saw that they were a vast multitude, which no one could number, from every nation, tribe, people, and language. The significance of the numbering lies in its depiction of an OT military census. John saw God's people in chapter 7 as an army and that is their function here as well. There remains, however, some debate as to whether this army represents the church universal or a particular group of martyrs whose death will result in the conversion of the nations.[37] While the idea of the 144,000 being martyrs is theologically justifiable, the fact that 144,000 are seen in chapter 7 as innumerable and are

[36] Wall 179
[37] For the universal church view see Beale, Keener, and Osborne. For the martyrs view see Caird, Reddish, and Bauckham.

spoken of in 14:3 as 'purchased from the earth,' it is more likely that they represent the entire body of Christ whenever they appear in John's vision.[38] It must be noted, as Mounce observes, that further significance of the number is to show that not one has been lost despite the conquering of the beasts.[39] As we will see shortly, the thing that "distinguishes these 144,000 from the rest of the human race is something very simple. They are able to learn a song."[40]

The image of God's people being marked on the forehead comes primarily from Ezekiel 9:4 where it depicts spiritual protection of the faithful remnant. Earlier in Rev. 3:12, Jesus promised to write he and his father's name on the faithful members of the church at Philadelphia. This happens in chapter 7, and later in v. 22:4 God's servants bear the name of God and the Lamb on their foreheads. While various meanings of the mark have been put forth[41], its primarily identifies the Lamb's army as opposed to those who have

[38] Beale sees the 144,000 as "the totality of God's people throughout the ages, viewed as true Israelites." He goes on to state that the name and seal are marks of genuine membership in the community of redeemed, without which entry into Zion is impossible. Therefore, entire community of redeemed, not just part. 733-735
[39] Mounce 268
[40] Michaels, Michaels, J. Ramsey. Revelation: IVP New Testament Commentary Series. InterVarsity, Downers Grove. 1997, p.168
[41] Barclay lists 5 primary meanings of the mark/seal in the ancient world: ownership, loyalty, security, dependence, and safety. 134-135

allied themselves with the Dragon and the Beasts.[42] It serves as a vivid contrast between the two camps: the earth dwellers have the name of the beast (in the numerical form 666) written on their foreheads while the soldiers of the Lamb have ὄνομα αὐτοῦ καὶ τὸ ὄνομα τοῦ πατρὸς αὐτοῦ written on theirs. It must also be pointed out that the believers' seal consisting of the names of the Lamb and of God "further extends the major theme of the book, the oneness of the Father and the Son."[43]

V. 2) John next hears a φωνὴν ἐκ τοῦ οὐρανοῦ. Many have translated φωνὴν as 'voice' because elsewhere in Revelation voices sound like ὑδάτων πολλῶν καὶ ὡς φωνὴν βροντῆς μεγάλης (1:15, 19:6). However, since the φωνὴν includes the sound of harps, which accompany the 'new song' in v.4, it is better to render it simply as 'sound.' The onomatopoeic phrase κιθαρῳδῶν κιθαριζόντων ἐν ταῖς κιθάραις αὐτῶν resembles Hebrew syntactical construction whereby the verb and the direct object are the same word (i.e. גְּדֹלָה חֲטָאָה חֲטָאתֶם Ex. 32:30). Wall sees the mentioning of rushing waters and harps as being melodious[44], while

---

[42] Beale feels that the 666 on the foreheads of beast's followers connotes their incompleteness in achieving the divine design for humanity. 733

[43] Osborne, Grant. Revelation: ECNT. Baker, Grand Rapids. 2002, p.526

[44] Wall 179

Osborne sees it as a boisterous celebration.[45] (Aune deems vv.2-3 a later addition to the text[46]—a conclusion with little, if any, textual evidence for such an addition.) The fact that the sound originates from heaven, "clearly distinguishing between Mount Zion and heaven"[47] leads many commentators to view this as an earthly celebration rather than a heavenly one. While this is possible, it should be noted that if John were to witness a heavenly celebration on a heavenly Zion, to him the sound would still appear to be coming from heaven.

V.3) The sound that John hears is the sound of the new song being sung by the '144,000 who had been purchased from the earth.' Commentators differ as to the source of the song—some seeing it as sung by God[48], others taking angels as the source.[49] However, there no good reason to think that those who have never been redeemed are teaching such a song to those who have.[50]

---

[45] Osborne 526
[46] "This entire section appears to have been inserted by the author into a larger, perhaps truncated, version of a traditional unit that dealt with the Messiah's appearance on Mount Zion, followed by the decisive defeat of his enemies and the gathering of his people." Aune 806
[47] Aune 803
[48] Barclay 137
[49] Johnson 537
[50] Morris, Leon. The Revelation of St. John. Tyndale, London. 1969, p.176

216

Throughout the Psalms[51], the 'new song' is a hymn of praise for the fact that YHWH has delivered his people as a call to the saints to put their trust in him completely.[52] This is the 3rd of 4 hymns in the book of Revelation and as Osborne observes, there is a natural progression in the four hymns: 5:9 celebrates the purchase of people by the blood of Christ; 14:2-3 celebrates the victory of the saints over the beast; 15:2-4 celebrates the justice of God in the final judgment plagues; and 19:6-7 celebrates the messianic wedding feast.[53] Isaiah prophesied of an eschatological celebration, complete with singing and taking place on Mt. Zion, by those who had been 'ransomed of YHWH' (Isa 35:10)[54]. No doubt the 'new song' John hears in ch.14, in conjunction with the other three hymns in his Apocalypse, is the final fulfillment of Isaiah's prophecy.

Noting that this is the only place in Revelation where a song is mentioned but not quoted, Aune feels that the fact that the author does not provide a transcript of the new song suggests that since he is not part of the 144,000, he himself cannot understand the

---

[51] See Psa. 33:3, 96:1, 98:1, 144:9, 149:1
[52] Osborne 527
[53] Osborne 526
[54] cf. Isa. 42:10

song.[55] This is an argument from silence that is not forced upon us by the text. Osborne is probably more accurate in stating that the reason the new song can only be learned by the 144,000 is because it is the highest worship in heaven and therefore, can only be sung by those victorious heaven-dwellers who have overcome the deceptions of the false trinity.[56] If John were to record the words, anyone who read his account, even τοὺς καθημένους ἐπὶ τῆς γῆς would be able to learn the song without having experienced its contents. Looking back to the previous chapters, we can now see that believers who could not purchase anything because they didn't have the mark of the beast have now been purchased "by the blood of the Lamb and bear his mark. The redeemed community is a worshipping celebrating community that learns the new song of the new age.[57] Caird puts it quite eloquently when he says, "For this song would be compounded of agony and groans, transmuted by the mysterious power of the Cross into the harmonies of heaven."[58]

---

[55] Aune 808-809. Aune does correctly observe that 'oi` hvgorasme,noi avpo. th/j gh/j' could either mean 'purchased from all parts of the world' or 'redeemed from the place of unbelief.'
[56] Osborne 527
[57] Boring 168
[58] Caird, G.B. Caird, G.B. The Revelation of Saint John: Black's New Testament Commentary. Hendrickson, Peabody. 1999, p.179

218

V.4) The phrases οἳ μετὰ γυναικῶν οὐκ ἐμολύνθησαν and παρθένοι γάρ εἰσιν are seen by the majority of scholars as the most difficult phrases in this passage, and possibly even in the entire book. Is John claiming that only men will be purchased from the earth and join the Lamb in heavenly celebration—and only virgins at that? Commentators have offered three basic interpretations of this verse:[59] 1) The 144,000 are to be seen as literal male virgins[60], 2) the 144,000's celibacy is seen as symbolic of spiritual purity[61], 3) the 144,000 are the Lamb's end-time army and are seen as obeying Holy War regulations.[62] Barclay takes the phrases literally, stating that the passage does not read as if it were metaphorical.[63] However, he realizes that a literal interpretation puts this passage in conflict with the rest of the NT, which teaches that marital sex is not defiling or sinful. He is forced by his literal interpretation to conclude that οἳ μετὰ γυναικῶν οὐκ ἐμολύνθησαν, and παρθένοι γάρ εἰσιν were originally marginal

---

[59] Osborne notes that some have seen this verse as a contrast to the angels in Gen. 6:1-4 who defiled themselves with women. (Osborne 529). Besides not being widely held, this view assumes that Gen. 6 depicts supernatural beings having sexual relationships with human women. However, many scholars (including this author) do not see this as a correct interpretation Gen. 6.

[60] Barclay holds this view.

[61] Examples of commentators who hold to some form of this view are Osborne, Beale, Mounce, Aune, Ladd, Morris, and Wall.

[62] Caird, Bauckham, Boring, Michaels, Keener, and Reddish all put forth this interpretation.

[63] Barclay 138

notes added by an ascetic copyist that found their way into the text itself.[64] However, not only does this conclusion lack any textual evidence, but it also fails to take into account the sexual symbolism of the rest of the book, as well as Scripture in general. Beale points out that if 144,000 is a figurative number for completeness, why should not the mention of "virgins" also be figurative in like manner?[65] He and other scholars point to the frequent use of sexual immorality to portray spiritual idolatry whereas virginity portrays spiritual purity. John, they claim, is picking up on the theme of Israel being pictured as a virgin in the OT[66] and the church likewise spoken of in the NT.[67] Therefore, according to Osborne, the παρθένοι are "those who refused to participate not only in immorality but in worldly pursuits of all kinds. With the imagery of the bride of the Lamb in 19:7-8 and 21:2, the idea of the virgin bride would make a great deal of sense."[68] Beale agrees and sees the idea of celibates as part of a picture of those who have not had illegitimate intercourse with the "great harlot" in 17:1.[69] Wall agrees with a figurative interpretation, noting that γυναικῶν are to be associated with the evil women in

---

[64] Ibid 140-141
[65] Beale 739
[66] 2 Kings 19:21,Isaiah 37:22, Jeremiah 14:17, 18:13, 31:4
[67] 2 Corinthians 11:2
[68] Osborne, 529
[69] Beale 740

Revelation, i.e. Jezebel in ch.2 and the Prostitute ch.17.[70] Noting the masculine παρθένοι, Michaels feels that reason they are seen here as male is because they were seen back in ch.7 as "sons of Israel."[71] He then states, "corporately they are seen as female because they will be the Bride of Christ. While strange to us, Revelation echoes Galatians 3:28 "no longer male nor female for all are one in Christ Jesus."[72] The notion of παρθένοι being figurative is undoubtedly correct, however other scholars see a different kind of symbolism in the phrase. Since the 144,000 were first seen in a military manner in chapter 7, the idea of their not being 'defiled with women' comes from the fact that in wartime, soldiers in the Israelite army were to abstain from sex or else they would be unclean.[73] Since the idea of holy war is prominent in the Apocalypse, and especially since the war against the saints was so prominent in chapter 13, this idea of celibacy most likely refers to Israelite military

[70] Wall 180
[71] Michaels 170
[72] Ibid 171-172
[73] cf. 1 Samuel 21:5. The Qumran community also held to this standard for their end-time army code. We find in 1QM 7:1-6 that only men 25 years old or older will be permitted to be part of God's end-time army and that if they have not "cleansed their 'spring' on the day of battle" they will not be allowed to go down with the army, "for the holy angels are together with their armies" and "no immodest nakedness will be seen in the surroundings of all their camps."

regulation.[74]   Boring agrees with the military metaphor and eve links the notion of celibacy to the Levitical regulations for those serving as priests, stating that since John pictures the church as the army of God and as priests, it is therefore pictured as a community of chaste 'virgins.'[75] It is most likely that the references to celibacy refer to both spiritual purity and the notion of an end-time army preparing for battle.   Both of these themes are prevalent throughout John's apocalypse.   As Keener states, "a spiritual celibate set aside for God cannot sleep with the world 'on the side' and remain qualified for God's triumphant army."[76]

Not only are God's people pictured as a spiritually pure end-times army, they are also referred to as οἱ ἀκολουθοῦντες τῷ ἀρνίῳ ὅπου ἂν ὑπάγῃ. This is a clear reference to Jesus' words in John 10:4: "*When he has brought out all his own, he goes before them, and the sheep follow him, for they know his voice.*"   This following not refer to following the Lamb as it wanders around heaven; it refers to the Lamb's followers following him in his suffering.   Caird feels that the best commentary on this verse is John 13:36: "*Simon Peter said to him, 'Lord, where are you*

[74] Osborne 529
[75] Boring 169
[76] Keener 380

going?' Jesus answered him, 'Where I am going you cannot follow me now, but you will follow afterward.'" Peter could not follow at that time because "Jesus was going to that death which was the salvation of the world and the glorification of the Son of Man...Only when on the Cross he had drawn all men, Peter included, into unity with himself, could Peter follow him on the road to self sacrificing love."[77]

And not only are the 144,000 seen as a celibate army who followed the Lamb wherever he goes, they are also seen as ἀπαρχὴ τῷ θεῷ καὶ τῷ ἀρνίῳ. The notion of 'firstfruits' can mean two things: 1) the 144,000 are the first wave of martyrs whose deaths will bring about the salvation of many more[78] or 2) the 144,000 are the firstfruits of the new creation.[79] Reddish claims that the 144,000 are the first fruits, the first of the offerings to God and the rest of the redeemed will complete the offering.[80] Caird agrees, and feels that the sacrificial language implies that they are to win "an innumerable host of converts."[81] This would mean that while the 144,000 represent the whole church at the

---

[77] Caird 179
[78] Caird, Bauckham, and Reddish are advocates of this interpretation.
[79] This view is held by Beale, Osborne, Barclay, and Ladd.
[80] Reddish 275
[81] Caird 188

time, in the end their numbers will increase significantly. While not completely implausible, this view doesn't seem to fit with the concept in chapter 7 of the 144,000 being synonymous with the entire host of the redeemed. However, if in chapter 7 the multitude is seen as the final result of the 144,000's ironic victory through martyrdom, then there is no inherent contradiction.

Picking up on the reference in James 1:18 to believers as 'firstfruits of creation,' other commentators see the 144,000 marking the beginning of the new creation in Christ.[82] Beale notes that the language of firstfruits in the OT is used to describe the first and best of one's produce being offered to YHWH. The rest of the produce after the firstfruits was considered "common or profane, and so now the redeemed are specially set apart from the rest, which are unclean, common, or profane."[83] Barclay agrees stating: "Each individual Christian is a foretaste of the time when all the world will be dedicated to God; and the Christian is the man who has consecrated and dedicated his life to God."[84] By this interpretation, the 144,000 are the best and finest that the world has to offer. In

---

[82] Osborne 530 cf. Beale 744
[83] Beale 744
[84] Barclay 142

light of the next verse, this view is more likely accurate.

V.5) The final thing John notices about the 144,000 is that οὐχ εὑρέθη ψεῦδος in their mouth and that they are ἄμωμοί. Throughout the OT deceit and lying are held in utter contempt, whereas truthfulness is seen as one of the highest virtues.[85] Aune points out that ἐν τῷ στόματι αὐτῶν οὐχ εὑρέθη ψεῦδος is a semitic idiom for telling the truth. And by the late 2nd Temple period, God was associated with truth and Satan with lies.[86] Zephaniah prophesied concerning God's end-time people: "*those who are left in Israel; they shall do no injustice and speak no lies, nor shall there be found in their mouth a deceitful tongue. For they shall graze and lie down, and none shall make them afraid (Zeph. 3:13)."* John's vision is the fulfillment of this prophecy and it further illustrates how the followers of the Lamb are imitators of their leader, for in Isaiah's prophecy of the suffering servant, we are told that he suffered "*although he had done no violence and there was no deceit in his mouth (Isa. 53:9)."* Beale feels that what is in mind here is not merely general truthfulness, but the saints' integrity in witnessing to Jesus when they are under

---

[85] cf. Psalm 32:2, 40:4
[86] Aune 823

pressure from the beast and the "false prophet" to compromise their faith and go along with the idolatrous lie.[87]

God's end-time army is also called ἄμωμοι. This term is used both to describe sacrifices offered to God as well as ethical or moral blamelessness.[88] Because ἄμωμοι can have both meanings, scholars differ as to its meaning here.[89] Noting the term's sacrificial connotation, Beal claims that ἄμωμοι is referring here not to absolute moral perfection but to innocence with regard to the world's verdict of guilt rendered against the saints, which he argues is the main point of Isa. 53:7-9.[90] Boring, likewise sees neither of these statements as a moralistic description of the church's piety. Rather, their refusal to lie means their resistance to the idolatrous propaganda of the false prophet, the master of the lie, "blameless" is the "character of a sacrifice, as their martyr's deaths were understood to be."[91] However, it must be noted that when used of believers in the NT,

---

[87] Beale 746

[88] For sacrificial nuance cf. Num. 7:88, 28:19, 28:31, 29:13, 1 Pet 1:19, Heb 9:14. For ethical/moral meaning cf. Psa 118:1, Pro 11:20, Ephesians 1:4, 5:27, Philippians 2:15, Colossians 1:22, 2 Peter 1:19, and Jude 1:24.

[89] Beale, Boring, and Reddish see it as symbolic purity while Osborne, Mounce, and Aune opt for literal moral blamelessness.

[90] Beale 747

[91] Boring 168

226

ἄμωμοι uniformly means ethically blameless.[92] This leads other scholars to conclude that in this passage the 144,000 are without moral blemish. Anticipating anti-perfectionist arguments, Osborne clarifies: "Of course, this does not entail absolute perfection but rather a total walk with Christ and an absolute commitment to God, in keeping with its use elsewhere in the NT."[93] The view that ἄμωμοι is a description of the moral state of the 144,000 finds much support elsewhere in the NT. However, it is clearly a sacrificial term as well. In fact, the latter use gave rise to the former. Therefore in John's vision, the 144,000 are portrayed as a sacrifice without blemish precisely because no lie is found in their mouth—they have kept themselves from being tainted by the seductions of the earth-dwellers and have overcome the persecution unholy trinity by living lives that are wholly devoted to the Lamb and refusing to compromise in any way. This may be hard for the modern Christian reader to understand due to the prevalence of sin among those who claim to follow Christ. Nonetheless, in John's vision that is what we are confronted with.

[92] Mounce 271
[93] Osborne 531

Conclusion:

Revelation 14:1-5 is primarily a depiction of the hope that all Christians can cling to, specifically those who are being persecuted for their obedience to Jesus and their refusal to play by the rules of an ungodly society. John presents his readers with a vision of the escatalogical celebration that awaits everyone who belongs to the army of the Lamb. Though they have suffered greatly under the tyranny of Satan and his minions, they will burst forth in ecstatic praise of their Lord who delivered them safely to Mt. Zion, keeping them pure and unblemished by his presence among them. However, for someone who has not been purchased from the earth by the blood of the Lamb the content of this celebration will remain a mystery and they will suffer the judgment portrayed in the rest of the chapter.

Sources:

Aune, David E.   Word Biblical Commentary, Vol.52b: Revelation 6-16.   Thomas Nelson, Nashville. 1998.

Barclay, William.   The Revelation of John, Vol.2. Westminster, Philadelphia. 1960.

Bauckham, Richard. The Theology of the Book of Revelation. Cambridge, Cambridge. 2002

Beale, G.K.   The New International Greek Testament   Commentary: Revelation. Eerdmans, Grand Rapids. 1999.

Boring, Eugene M. Revelation: Interpretation. John Knox, Louisville. 1989.

Caird, G.B.   The Revelation of Saint John: Black's   New   Testament   Commentary. Hendrickson, Peabody. 1999.

Johnson, Alan.   "Revelation." The Expositor's Bible Commentary, Vol.12. Zondervan, Grand Rapids. 1981.

Keener, Craig S.   Revelation: The NIV Application Commentary. Zondervan, Grand Rapids. 2000.

Ladd, George Eldon. A Commentary on The Revelation of John. Eerdmans, Grand Rapids. 1972.

Martinez, Florentio Garcia. The Dead Sea Scrolls: Study Edition. Eerdmans, Grand Rapids. 1997.

Michaels, J. Ramsey. Revelation: IVP New Testament Commentary Series. InterVarsity, Downers Grove. 1997.

Morris, Leon. The Revelation of St. John. Tyndale, London. 1969.

Mounce, Robert H. The Book of Revelation: The New International Commentary on the New Testament. Eerdmans, Grand Rapids. 1977.

Osborne, Grant R. Revelation: Baker Exegetical Commentary on the New Testament. Baker, Grand Rapids. 2002.

Reddish, Mitchell G. Revelation: Smyth & Helwys Bible Commentary. Smyth & Helwys, Macon. 2001.

Wall, Robert W. Revelation: New International Biblical Commentary. Hendrickson, Peabody. 1991.

About the Author

James-Michael Smith (M.Div, *Gordon-Conwell Theological Seminary*) is a Bible teacher, speaker and author who teaches seminars and short-term Biblical Studies, Christian Thought and Theology courses in local churches and ministries. He is also an occasional speaker at *CharlotteONE:* (www.charlotteone.org), a citywide worship gathering of young adults in the metro Charlotte area. After serving as Discipleship Pastor in the local church setting for 5 years, he founded Disciple Dojo in order to help equip Christians with the resources needed to encourage their own spiritual growth as well as to engage the surrounding culture with the Gospel of Jesus.

JM's random "about the author" facts:

* My theological influences are as varied as John Wesley, N.T. Wright, Ben Witherington III, Alister McGrath, Watchman Nee, Ravi Zacharias, Gordon Fee, Doug Stuart, D.A. Carson, C.S. Lewis, Walt Kaiser and William Wilberforce.

* I was raised in the inner-city in Savannah, GA where my Father (also a Gordon-Conwel grad!) was Pastor of Inner City United Methodist Church, a small storefront church ministering primarily to residents the surrounding housing projects.

* I'm a trained artist with a degree in Drawing/Painting and have been able to combine my art with ministry in a variety of ways including live paintings on stage during worship/sermons, graphic design of all my teaching resources and website artwork, and lobby mural design at Good Shepherd UMC in Charlotte, NC.

* I'm a lifelong martial artist with a Black Belt in from Sensei Derek Richardson at Leadership Martial Arts, Charlotte, NC and currently a Blue Belt in Brazilian Jiujitsu. I've had the privilege of training under and alongside some of the greatest martial artists in the world, including current and former UFC champions (which you can read about by subscribing to http://jmsmith.org/blog) and my favorite metaphor to describe the life of Christian Discipleship is that of the Samurai of feudal Japan.

* I love geeky documentaries on Discovery Channel and the History Channel, especially the ones about astronomy and theoretical physics concepts, despite having practically zero mathematic abilities. My favorite TV show of all time is The Simpsons and my favorite movie is "Big Trouble in Little China." I listen mostly to Jazz and profanity-free Hip Hop more and my favorite outdoor activity by far is snowboarding.

What Others Have Said About
JM and Disciple Dojo

"James-Michael's "Bible for the Rest of Us" was an excellent experience. It was better than some of my seminary classes. James-Michael combines a heart for God and intimate knowledge of his word with a high capacity to teach with humor, wit and simplicity. Its a real treat for anyone interested in an approach to learn more about the Bible on its own terms."

Rev. Rich Tuttle – Senior Pastor, Catawba United Methodist Church

----

"As a pastor for over 20 years I don't consider myself jaded to the word of God taught by other teachers and pastors by any stretch of the imagination, but I must say it can feel at times like many of the messages I hear just run together. Not so with James-Michael Smith! Refreshing, cutting edge and thought provoking are just a few ways in which I would describe the deep and life-altering teaching he delivers to the body of Christ. In fact I have a list of my top ten messages and recently one of his teachings made it into a top place on my list and almost blew the lid off! "The Woman, the Dragon & the Cross" message (available for free download in the Disciple Dojo audio archive at http://jmsmith.org/store/audio) is a must hear. It rocked my world and I will never be the same again. Give James-Michael a look. You will not be disappointed."

Rev. Steve Wright - Pastor, Legacy Church

"James-Michael is the kind of bible scholar I like: solid in his evangelical commitments and yet willing to challenge some evangelical pre-suppositions. We need more like him as biblical scholarship moves ahead into the 21st Century."

Rev. Talbot Davis – Senior Pastor, Good Shepherd United Methodist Church

----

Standing on a firm theological foundation, James-Michael is able to clearly communicate the timeless truths of the Christian Faith in a way any listener can understand and appreciate.

David Hickman – Executive Director, CityONE: Network and CharlotteONE:

Printed in Dunstable, United Kingdom

68148444R00137